What Your Colleague

"In this age of responding to the effects of two enduring pandemics–COVID and racism–this book is a must-read. Lauren M. Wells gives educators a long overdue charge: STOP using deficit ideology to educate Black youth. Dr. Wells weaves large-scale research, historical events, ecological theory, and human experiences into a book of answers to fix racial inequities in schooling. I applaud her commitment to shifting to an 'emancipatory' and systemic paradigm for school reform. Brava!"

—Cheryl Holcomb-McCoy, PhD
Dean and Distinguished Professor of Education
American University, School of Education

"There Are No Deficits Here *is a call to interrupt the beliefs and dismantle the practices and policies that prevent Black children from thriving in schools. Simultaneously an honest indictment of the education system as well as an invitation to correct it, Lauren M. Wells calls on all of us who claim to be invested in the education of Black children to step up individually and collectively and dream the change we know is possible. Dr. Wells makes plain her own story and mission to improve education and encourages all of us to do the same."*

—Yolanda Sealey-Ruiz, PhD, Professor
Teachers College, Columbia University
Co-author of *Advancing Racial Literacies in Teacher Education: Activism for Equity in Digital Spaces*

"There is such a wide diversity of thought in education circles relative to what equity is and what equity is not. Much of this thought is so disjointed that it leaves the teacher who wants to be a true equity practitioner completely confused. Lauren M. Wells's new book, There Are No Deficits Here: Disrupting Anti-Blackness in Education *brings it all together. I consider this book an important must read for anyone in education working with Black children. "*

—Principal Baruti Kafele, Author and Creator
Virtual Assistant Principal Leadership Academy

"What was most striking about my first reading of There Are No Deficits Here *was the earnestness by which Lauren M. Wells exposes and confronts anti-Blackness in schools. In this instructive text, readers will learn from the many named and unnamed Black students, educators, activists, and intellectuals Dr. Wells invokes in her writing. Despite delineating the multiplicative ways schooling reinforces white supremacy, each chapter emanates hope. The narratives, theories, and empirical evidence presented highlight how everyone benefits from Black people's brilliance. Rooted in praxis, Dr. Wells offers guidance to those committed to disrupting the pernicious effects of racism—in all its mutations—on our children."*

—Mildred Boveda, EdD, Associate Professor
Penn State, College of Education

"Since the construction of race and race-based 'science,' anti-Blackness has insidiously permeated every aspect of our society, institutions, structures, and systems, ultimately resulting in individual, collective, and structural life-altering impacts; the education system is no exception. In There Are No Deficits Here: Disrupting Anti-Blackness in Education, *Lauren M. Wells expertly lays out the ways U.S. schools have proven to be bastions of anti-Blackness and ecosystems that reinforce, maintain, and feed the structure of racial capitalism and anti-Blackness. Dr. Wells's weaving of personal narratives, coupled with the structural analysis, helps us understand the ways individuals experience and connect the dots. In a world where Black children, their communities, and their families are seen as deficits and inconveniences, schools become concentrated places where this messaging can either reinforce these deficit perspectives of Black children and their families or affirm their humanity.* There Are No Deficits Here *compels us to confront the ways anti-Blackness permeates while providing a possible solution to how we may interrupt anti-Blackness in schools using a systems-based analysis and approach.* There Are No Deficits Here *is a challenge to us all–to get it right, to take a more critical and deeper look at the root causes that limit Black students in schools and beyond while asking us to build new systems that affirm them."*

—**Awo Okaikor Aryee-Price**, Executive Director
Education for Liberation Network

"Lauren M. Wells challenges readers to take our conversations about equity to the next level. Well-intentioned leaders and policymakers can maintain practices and policies that undermine student achievement and ruin our aspirations for equity. The good news is that the author provides practical advice for every teacher, leader, and policymaker. Good intentions, Dr. Wells demonstrates, are not enough. We need concrete actions to match our rhetoric. This powerful book will make readers confront the difference between their espoused beliefs and their continued tolerance of white supremacy and anti-Black practices. Don't just read this book–study it, reflect on it, and join a community-wide conversation that will make all of us reflect on the difference between our intentions and our actions."

—**Douglas Reeves**, Author
Fearless Schools

"This book is a rally call for all who know that Black student genius is alive, active, and well. Lauren M. Wells's work challenges the deficit, inequitable, spirit-murdering, and warehousing structure that we call school and calls for an Emancipatory Educational Ecosystem to take its place, which consciously connects every entity of the community in service of every Black student. In the spirit of Frederick Douglass, Harriet Tubman, Carter G. Woodson, James Baldwin, and other historic and modern liberators, this concept is bold and doable. As the founding executive director of the Coalition of Schools Educating Boys of Color, an organization that advances the affirmative social, emotional, cultural, and academic development of boys and young men of color, I believe this book resonates with our mission. It is the blueprint for sincere educational transformation and the gateway for Black student genius to grow and proliferate in schools and community. I encourage all who believe and support this same belief to add this book to your strategic action tool chest immediately. Onward and upward!"

—**Ron Walker**, Executive Director
Coalition of Schools Educating Boys of Color

"If what we do says more about what we believe than what we say we believe . . . then this book must serve as an essential guide to help us reimagine how our schools can fearlessly pursue high intellectual performance, joy, freedom, and a sense of connection and meaningful relationships for our Black and Brown students. We must, as Lauren M. Wells asks, look in the mirror, both individually and collectively, and fiercely reimagine and rewire communities, schools, and classrooms to be the ecosystems of equity and justice our children deserve."

—Risa Sackman, Director, U.S. Education
FHI 360

"Lauren M. Wells takes on a topic of profound importance to all of us: 'How can we as educators purposefully and intentionally contribute to activating the limitless potential in Black students?' Setting forth a framework of analysis to explain how we came to be where we are, and what we need to do to 'ignite the genius already within our students,' Dr. Wells issues a clarion call for us to believe in (and act to support) the innate intellect and talent of Black students as evidenced by their creativity and resilience. Affirming beliefs become policy, systems, and practice, which create educational ecosystems designed for Black children to thrive. Providing both history, analysis, concrete steps for action, and a deep love of and appreciation for the Black students she works with, Dr. Wells has written a heartfelt book for constructive change."

—Pam Allyn, Founder and CEO
Dewey

"Lauren M. Wells highlights the inequities Black children face in the American educational system. She provides opportunities for reflection throughout the book, and the examples shared are thought-provoking and relevant to the current climate in this country. Dr. Wells challenges educators to not simply acknowledge the disparities in education but to reflect on our bias and take action to move the educational system forward. All educators should read this book; this would be an excellent resource for a graduate-level course on social justice."

—Dr. Edith C. Banks, Founder and CEO
The Sunflower National, LLC

"For generations, Black students' dreams have been shattered by a U.S. education system functioning precisely as it was designed—to underestimate their potential and underinvest in their development. Lauren M. Wells offers a vital counter vision for this broken system and a roadmap to create a better one that brings together our Black students' identities, cultures, histories, and communities. Grounded in emancipatory educational principles, Dr. Wells's conception of culturally responsive–sustaining education transformation is a gift to our beloved community and all those seeking to address the present anti-Black education system."

—Cheryl Lowery, President and CEO
The Joseph & Evelyn Lowery Institute for Justice & Human Rights

THERE ARE NO DEFICITS HERE

Chaz

Madison,

Xavier, Caden,

Zipporah, Keith, Christian

Troy, Maya,

Yasmin, Elijah,

Jua, Ama,

and

every Black child

in every classroom

in every school

everywhere.

THERE ARE NO DEFICITS HERE

DISRUPTING ANTI-BLACKNESS IN EDUCATION

LAUREN M. WELLS

Foreword by YVETTE JACKSON
Afterword by RAS BARAKA

CORWIN

FOR INFORMATION:

Corwin
A SAGE Company
2455 Teller Road
Thousand Oaks, California 91320
(800) 233-9936
www.corwin.com

SAGE Publications Ltd.
1 Oliver's Yard
55 City Road
London EC1Y 1SP
United Kingdom

SAGE Publications India Pvt. Ltd.
Unit No 323-333, Third Floor, F-Block
International Trade Tower Nehru Place
New Delhi 110 019

SAGE Publications Asia-Pacific Pte. Ltd.
18 Cross Street #10-10/11/12
China Square Central
Singapore 048423

Vice President and Editorial Director: Monica Eckman
Program Director and Publisher: Dan Alpert
Content Development Manager: Lucas Schleicher
Content Development Editor: Mia Rodriguez
Senior Editorial Assistant: Natalie Delpino
Project Editor: Amy Schroller
Copy Editor: Karin Rathert
Typesetter: C&M Digitals (P) Ltd.
Proofreader: Lawrence W. Baker
Cover Designer: Gail Buschman
Marketing Manager: Melissa Duclos

Printed in Canada

Library of Congress Cataloging-in-Publication Data

Names: Wells, Lauren M., author.

Title: There are no deficits here: disrupting anti-blackness in education / Lauren M. Wells.

Description: Thousand Oaks, California: Corwin, 2024. | Includes bibliographical references and index.

Identifiers: LCCN 2023015712 | ISBN 9781071855898 (paperback) | ISBN 9781071855942 (epub) | ISBN 9781071855928 (epub) | ISBN 9781071855911 (pdf)

Subjects: LCSH: Racism in education—United States. | Educational equalization—United States. | Anti-racism—United States. | African Americans—Education—Social aspects.

Classification: LCC LC212.2 .W43 2024 | DDC 370.890973—dc23/eng/20230510

LC record available at https://lccn.loc.gov/2023015712

This book is printed on acid-free paper.

23 24 25 26 27 10 9 8 7 6 5 4 3 2 1

Contents

Website Contents

To download the above tools and resources related to *There Are No Deficits Here*, please visit the companion website at **http://resources.corwin.com/NoDeficitsHere**.

FOREWORD

By Yvette Jackson

Cognitive and neuroscience substantiate that we are **all** wired with the innate propensity for the development of strengths and high intellectual performances, the imperative for self-actualization, and the desire to make contributions. So why are the educational goals and practices for students of color void of these findings??? Just take a look at the vison and mission statements in the districts where these students predominate. Key terms that reflect belief in their potential like "thriving," "flourishing," "intellectual development" and "self-actualization" are noticeably absent!!

When the potential of students is viewed as valuable assets, programs, opportunities, and supports are created to mine for that potential. This was demonstrated in the 1950s when the United States felt the need to compete with Russia for dominance in the space program. It became an American imperative to create specialized programs to nurture science and math expertise. This interest spurred educational researchers to devise empirical studies to investigate tools for assessing the aptitude of students who might be considered to have "exceptional" abilities to better cultivate "gifted" scientists. The value placed on the potential of these students legitimized labeling only an identified few as "exceptional" and needing of "exceptional" or "gifted" programs" of enrichment and acceleration so their potential could thrive and flourish (Jackson, 2011).

At the same time, the Feds were allotting monetary assistance for the development of compensatory education programs designed to identify and remediate what were considered "weaknesses" of students designated as "disadvantaged" under funding designated as "Title I." Low scores of poor students that fell below the statewide Normal Curve Equivalency on norm-referenced tests were labeled as illustrative of cognitive deficiencies (Ginsberg, 1972; Levine & Bane, 1975). A steadfast result of this classification (correlating poverty with low scores on standardized tests indicating cognitive deficiencies) was the prejudging of the capacity of these students as limited and therefore considering or addressing the interrelation of factors (neurobiological, cognitive, emotional, and social) that affect development of their potential in any systematic way was unwarranted.

This blatant ignorance or denial of the reality of the impact of the interrelation of these factors on the cognitive development and learning of Black and brown students was never more apparent than during the Covid-19 pandemic when the lack of coordination among support agencies and the diminution of their services was blatantly exposed. Even after Covid safety precautions were identified and vaccines were created, schooling was severely interrupted due to the shortages among healthcare, childcare, and technology systems. Schools remained closed so long that learning growth in the districts of poor Black and brown students who were already struggling academically due to the lack of access to computers for learning prior to Covid-19 fell even further behind (The 74, 2022). This result has perpetuated the belief that these students are demonstrating a learning "deficit" rather than the more extensive lack of access and support that is their reality.

If there was belief in the innate potential of our students of color, discovering and cultivating their unique gifts, talents, and interests would be a needed requisite in their schooling and barriers to the fulfillment of this potential would be eradicated. We would not accept anything less than a system that would totally disrupt the cancerous affixing of the labeling of our students as "low"-performing entities responded to with designations to segregated, remedial program tracks. Instead, education and support agencies would be directed to implement pedagogy and support services that address our students as intellectual, creative beings waiting to excel and valued for the promise of contributions they could make to America. We would view educators not as instructors but as liberators who emancipate that excellence.

This has been Dr. Wells's mission and her raison d'être for writing *There Are No Deficits Here: Disrupting Anti-Blackness in Education*. Her experiences as a teacher, working in partnership with schools and districts, and in-depth research in the science of learning made blatantly apparent to her that the impact of the environment on the neurobiology and cognition of the brain goes beyond the four walls of the school and the pedagogical responses teachers provide. Her vast leadership experience at the school, district, and mayoral levels made apparent to her that barriers to student learning go even beyond factors like poverty and lack of access to needed nutrition and health services, stereotype threats associated with race or ethnicity (Noguera, 2008; Steele & Aronson, 2004), the feelings of failure, or the trauma of adverse childhood experiences to include barriers emanating from the system itself—such as marginalizing teaching mandates and restrictions from state education departments. These restrictions negate belief in or attention to the potential of both the students and their many competent, committed teachers, deny them access to enriching experiences, and replace them with limited, parochial instruction. Dr. Wells's astute systems thinking led her to two critical recognitions: (1) schools are ecosystems that do not exist outside of the communities where they are located or the families whose children they educate; and (2) every level of the educational system has a direct impact on the learning and achievement of each and every student.

These recognitions led Dr. Wells to the realization that schools are ecosystems within ecosystems that interact with each other. This inspired her to build on ecosystems theory research to ingeniously curate a truly transformative model for educating students that eclipses the restrictive boundaries of the traditional American educational system. She demonstrates the importance of coherence and synergy within and across schools, communities, and support agencies to create learning environments that catalyze quantum learning growth and unearth the giftedness of our children as well as the productivity of the adults upon whom they depend.

Dr. Wells says her book provides us an invitation to look into the mirror, both individually and collectively, with the "hard-eyed view" required to fiercely reimagine communities, schools, and classrooms so that they are wired to be the ecosystems of equity and justice Black and brown children deserve. *There Are No Deficits Here: Disrupting Anti-Blackness in Education* is a Rosetta Stone that deftly translates pertinent concepts like the *ecology of equity* and *culturally responsive-sustaining education* into pedagogical practices that engage students' intellect and learning and provides invaluable resources for reculturating the school community such as the research on the science of belief, a *Belief Assessment Tool*, and exercises for introspection that can be assets for professional and community development.

There Are No Deficits Here: Disrupting Anti-Blackness in Education is a tour de force that will animate belief in the possibilities for a truly equitable education system committed to drawing out, valuing, and cultivating the innate potential of Black students for "high intellectual performances" and empowerment.

Acknowledgments

Everything happens in its time. I am grateful this book chose me at this time and grateful to the Creator for providing everything I needed at exactly the right time.

To those named and unnamed who struggled for centuries so I could use my voice.

To my maternal grandmother, Verna, for giving the women in our family the spirit of protest and power of voice and for planting the seeds of faith that give me a spiritual life today.

My Mama, also known as Mom, Mama Nat, Punch, and Natalie to the many who have devoured her biscuits, listened to her stories, and picked flowers or greens from her garden. This book, all that I do, is only possible because of the purpose and intentionality with which you curated my exposure to words, books, education, experiences, and people early in my life. I am so appreciative of your unwavering support for me and your faith in my personal journey. Thank you for your unconditional love. I love you without end.

To my sister, Sharon, you are the greatest symbol of strength and belief in my life. I hope you see your gifts as an educator reflected in this book. I love you for being my sister.

Bill, you are the most solid and gracious godfather anyone could hope to have. I thank you for being present in this process.

To those who gave me love, encouragement, motivation, and space like you couldn't imagine over the last two years. I could not have done this without you. Thank you. Tai, you believed in this book from the very first word. Jheryn and Linda, for celebrating small wins. Emily, for forty years of downloads and unfiltered conversation. Jerry, Toni, Mark, Leslie, and Niki, for reading chapters and asking questions that needed to be asked. Nelly, for listening to my doubts and worries without judgment. Tyra and Dana, for texts and check-ins. Eion, for being a real partner. Kai, for burgers, writing space, and spontaneous chats about all things and no things. Alturrick, for random banter coupled with all things political. Jason, for getting me over the finish line.

Tai, LaMont, Lauren, Larry, and Ms. Nelms, you helped me get the first chapters out. I really needed that! Bree and Risa, your generous and incredibly valuable feedback helped the book along immensely. Rosemary, thank you for providing a place to write.

Okaikor, we met for coffee on a cloudy morning and you invited me to join Homeroom. I will never be able to fully share how that act of care shaped my writing and helped me grow. I am forever grateful to you for inviting me to this space.

My deepest gratitude to Homeroom for accepting me into the loving and powerful community you have created. I have no doubt that this space gave me courage, insights, and stamina to finish. You embody the power of the intellect and sisterhood of Black womanhood magnificently! Mildred, thank you for sharing resources, insights, fierceness, and just straight encouragement at the right time. Okaikor, thank you for your precision and discerning eye.

To my community. I am blessed to be among you. We ain't perfect. We disagree. But there is something about looking across a room and seeing someone you know you can count on, knowing unequivocally where they stand. We work hard to empower ourselves. We've lost important people in our struggle too soon. For Roberto and Ms. Holder, we speak your names.

Barbara, Jim, Joanne, Zaquia, Roy, Erskine, and Ras. All the Global Village students, teachers, administrators, families, community leaders, and partners. Carolota, Eddie, Barika, and Trevor, thank you for working with and facing challenges with me. Thank you Jeannie and Pedro, for giving me the opportunity to lead BBA in Newark. In memory of Dr. Clifford Janey, who created the opportunity for us all to generate change and be changed by the work.

To NPS, you have been my teacher and partner for longer than I could have imagined. It is a privilege to be a witness to your triumphs, aspirations, and challenges and to be embraced as a critical friend. Thank you for giving me the opportunity to support and strive with you.

Thank you to the teachers, principals, and administrators who have partnered with me for your confidence and partnership. I take nothing for granted. May this book be helpful to you in the ways you need it to be.

Yvette, you are the *Pedagogy of Confidence!* Thank you for pushing me to write this on my own and for making your belief my belief. Thank you for contributing to my development and this book.

Ras, I am so pleased your voice in present in this book. I have been privileged to evolve these ideas in our work to change schools.

Thank you for demonstrating to us all that we are never one thing, that we can be right and wrong, a leader and artist all at once.

Yolanda, thank you for your inspiration, support, and encouragement from the first time we met.

I would also like to offer my deepest gratitude to Zaretta Hammond and Bettina Love for sharing your genius and powerful ideas with us. Though I do not know you personally, your work has influenced me profoundly.

To those who reviewed an early draft of the manuscript for this book, thank you. In some cases your feedback helped me to clarify why I was struggling in certain places and, in others, it affirmed I was headed someplace people may not want to go but definitely need to.

I am deeply appreciative to and for my therapist, Nancy, for focusing me, challenging me, and giving me tools to work through my own beliefs about myself and to become more masterful of my thoughts and actions.

My editor, Dan Alpert, believed in the book from the beginning, coached me, and supported the ideas and concepts as they evolved and came together. Dan, I am so thankful for the clarity with which you saw and understood me and this book. Lucas Schleicher, you were a Godsend. Thank you for your incisive eyes and ability to pull out the ideas and meanings I buried. I have so much gratitude for you both for supporting this expression of the connections that have lived inside of me. Thank you to everyone at Corwin who helped this book finds its ways into educators' hands.

Writing this book is the most liberating thing I have ever done. I own my story, my voice, and my purpose.

May the ancestors be pleased with me.

PUBLISHER'S ACKNOWLEDGMENTS

Corwin gratefully acknowledges the contributions of the following reviewers:

Peter Dillon, EdD
Superintendent of Schools
Berkshire Hills Regional School District / Richmond
Consolidated School
Stockbridge, MA

Risa Sackman
Director, US Education
FHI 360
Washington, DC

About the Author

Lauren M. Wells, PhD, is an educator, researcher, and community organizer whose work centers on comprehensive, systemic, racially just, and collaborative approaches to educational and social change. She began her work in education over twenty years ago while an undergraduate student at Temple University. Her experiences as a high school teacher led her on a quest to create schools that are designed to work for and elevate Black and brown students and their communities. Lauren is trained in qualitative research and uses an interdisciplinary approach to understanding the social problems confronting communities and schools. She applies this approach not only to the work of school transformation but also to transforming how communities, educators, and policymakers think about, approach, and engage in educational and social transformation. Wells has been at the forefront of education policy and transformation in New Jersey for over fifteen years.

In 2009, Lauren became the director of the Broader Bolder Approach to Education at the Metropolitan Center for Urban Education at New York University (NYU), where she led the design and implementation of a major school reform initiative in Newark called the "Newark Global Village School Zone." This reform has had a lasting impact on Central High School, one of Newark's comprehensive high schools. She has served as chief education officer for Mayor Ras Baraka in the City of Newark, where she led education policy and developed initiatives on behalf of the city, and a professor of education at the University of Southern California, Montclair State University, and American University. She is currently an Equity in Action Presidential Fellow at Kean University. In 2016, Lauren founded Creed Strategies, LLC, to create a community of consultants whose core mission is to use their knowledge, experience, and resources to work alongside educators and communities to ignite conditions for equity and justice. Lauren has worked in school districts across the nation on educational equity and school transformation as well as with philanthropy, nonprofit organizations, and public advocacy. A committed community advocate, Lauren serves on several boards and participates in community coalitions. From 2014 to 2019, Lauren was chair of the Newark Youth Policy Board. Lauren is currently entering her fourth term as president of the Newark Public Library Board.

Lauren received a BA in English from Temple University, an MA in educational leadership from Teachers College, Columbia University, and a PhD in educational policy from the University of California, Los Angeles.

Introduction

Discussing herein the mistakes made in the education of the Negro, the writer frankly admits he has committed some of these errors himself.

—Carter G. Woodson

Not everything that is faced can be changed, but nothing can be changed until it is faced.

—James Baldwin

More time. More basic skills. More discipline. More social-emotional learning. More core content. More testing. More data. More grit. These are among some of the leading refrains about what is needed to improve the academic performance of students of color—Black students in particular—or to close the so-called "achievement gap." But essentially, all these refrains call for more of the same and assume our prevailing educational paradigm is sound. Give it a tweak here. A new program there. Add a little special sauce. Sprinkle a few data points on top. Voilà, a silver bullet.

The assumption that our educational system is good, just a little broken, has vexed me throughout my professional journey as an educator. Whether in the classroom, supporting school and district leaders, partnering with community-based organizations, working with aspiring school leaders, or developing initiatives at the municipal level, this assumption has dominated both outlooks about education and approaches to addressing the "savage inequalities" that persist at every level and in every aspect of our educational ecosystems. The foundation, the structure, and the roots remain unquestioned and unchallenged. And the resulting policies, programs, curricula, and reforms act more like trickle-down education than educational transformation. Maybe it's because we can't see the structure or the foundation of something that's been built. Or we can't see the roots once a seed has been planted. But I can see apartheid learning conditions. I can see curricula and textbooks. I can see pedagogy. I can see seating arrangements and discipline and suspensions. I can see parents and communities disregarded. I can see the evidence of the structure and the foundation and the roots on the walls of classrooms, in the halls of schools, and in the eyes of Black students who feel unseen. I can see.

Education, literacy specifically, has always been valued in the lives of Black people. We have used it to name, navigate, contest, and fight against oppression and injustice in our lives and, at times, at great peril (Douglas, 2020; Muhammad, 2020; Perry et al., 2004). During Reconstruction, Black freedmen's organizations created and supported independent schools for Black children, which led the way toward universal education (Anderson, 1983). The desegregation of schools was central to the civil rights movement. In the 1970s, Black college students organized across college campuses for Black studies courses and campus diversity. Today, communities across the nation form coalitions, alliances, and build movements to demand educational opportunities for Black children and other children of color that are equitable, socially just, and culturally responsive and sustaining. But the failure of education reform to address the potency and saliency of white supremacy, anti-Blackness, and other deficit beliefs that flow from society into our laws, policies, and practices and ultimately into our schools and classrooms persists. After so much reform, there has been so little change (Payne, 2013). An education system that is so inherently inequitable cannot be the "great equalizer" it is narrated to be.

My sister and I grew up surrounded by civil rights activists and social justice messages. My mother talked to us about her activism as a college student at Pennsylvania State University, where she belonged to a group of Black students who are responsible for the creation of the Paul Robeson Cultural Center at Penn State's University Park Campus in 1972. The students held protests, circulated petitions, and sat-in at the president's office to demand a space where Black students could gather to celebrate, affirm, and support Black history and issues. My mother never diminished the anger she and the other Black students felt about the lack of Black professors, the racist comments and lessons they encountered from white faculty, or the limited courses about Black history and culture available to them. But the pride with which she shared the outcomes of their demonstrations and meetings with campus administration also communicated the importance of acting. Sundays spent at Central United Methodist Church in Atlanta, Georgia, during the late 1970s and early 1980s reinforced these messages from my mother. As I child, I was in awe of Central's pastor, Dr. Joseph Lowery. You see, Dr. Lowery, a civil rights leader, preached unapologetic sermons about Black liberation and God being with those who fight for justice. His sermons taught me to see injustice and be committed to fight against it.

I can see that white supremacy and anti-Blackness produce toxic educational cultures that steal the belonging, purpose, pride, and joy that learning should give all students from Black students. Our system of education is saturated with anti-Black policies, content, and practices that create "survival" conditions and marginal learning opportunities that are unique to the experiences of Black students (Dumas, 2016). Black students—Black people—are not monolithic in America or anywhere in the world. "Racialized physical markers create common experiences of social marginalization" for Black students, families, and communities from all ethnic backgrounds (Hernández, 2022). We, of course, all have multiple and intersecting identities. Yet because living at the intersection of a Black racial identity powerfully impacts our experiences and outcomes in every sphere of social life, this book focuses on Black students—American born, African, Afro-Caribbean, Afro-Latino/a, and other Black students from the African diaspora.

The harmful educational experiences Black students endure make me angry. For a long time, I felt ashamed for my anger or, more precisely, the expressions of my anger that others felt should be tempered. Now, I affirm my anger and that of others who courageously refuse to participate passively in oppressive systems, structures, or practices. But as my mother, Dr. Lowery, and the lives of so many activists today convey—being angry is necessary but insufficient. So the question for me and the work we do as educators is, "How do we understand inequities in public education as the intended consequences of the anti-Blackness inherent in American society and collectively work toward emancipatory educational ecosystems designed for Black children to thrive?" This book is my attempt to address this question.

THE ORGANIZATION OF THE BOOK

Part I begins the book with a reflection on the personal and professional context in which the ideas, theories, and frameworks I provide have developed. In Chapter 1, I situate my entry into education as the foundation for my thinking about classrooms, schools, and districts as ecosystems and the role of beliefs about Black students in their learning experiences. I introduce emancipatory educational ecosystems to help us reconceptualize our thinking about the education we provide to Black students. Chapter 2 turns to examples of efforts to transform education in Newark, New Jersey, that contribute to my belief that affirming beliefs and capacity for culturally responsive-sustaining education (CRSE) are needed to create learning that elicits the genius of Black students. In Chapter 3, I offer conscious collectivism—a framework for the continuous partnership with all stakeholders to work together to intentionally create the emancipatory educational ecosystems Black students deserve.

After exploring the context in which my understanding evolved, Part II examines the collective context of our prevailing educational paradigm, what educational scholar Love (2019) calls the "educational survival complex." I consider the intersections of social systems and racial ideologies and Bronfenbrenner's (2005) ecological systems theory, a widely held explanation for the influence of the social environment on children and human development, and build on Jackson (2010) and Hammond's (2015) work about culture and the brain. Chapter 4 considers Covid-19 and the murder of George Floyd as examples of the racialized social dynamics that exist in our society and looks to ecosystems in nature to establish the understanding that ecosystems, including our society, are governed by general principles. In Chapter 5, I discuss Bronfenbrenner's ecological system framework and consider its limitations for understanding how race operates in our society and educational ecosystems. Chapter 6 examines the influence of culture on our educational ecosystems and draws from my teaching and high school experiences to provide examples of Love's conceptualization of the "educational survival complex." The relationship between our beliefs and actions and how beliefs operate in our subconscious and conscious thinking is examined in Chapter 7, where I offer a brief look at new neuroscience research that is beginning to illuminate specific interactions between culture and our brains.

Part III moves us into collective purpose, the pursuit of emancipatory educational ecosystems for educating Black students (and all students in general), which requires we develop affirming beliefs and the knowledge and skills to undertake culturally responsive-sustaining educational transformation (CRSET). Chapter 8 introduces affirming beliefs that can help move your ecosystem toward emancipatory educational ecosystems where learning is connected to the identities, cultures, histories, and communities of Black students. Chapter 9 draws from leaders in the field of culturally responsive-sustaining education (CRSE) and uses insights from a culturally responsive education pilot in a district I call Hilltop to demonstrate the importance of CRSET to an emancipatory educational ecosystem.

Included in the chapters are *Pause and Process* sections that offer you opportunities to reflect and engage individually and collectively with the ideas and content I present. Each *Pause and Process* section begins with *Individual Reflection* and moves into *Collective Planning*. This allows flexibility in how the sections are utilized. For example, if you are reading together as a school, the *Individual Reflection* can be completed independently at home and the *Collectively Planning* during the PLC or other meeting time when you come together to discuss the book. The interaction of *Individual Reflection* and *Collective Planning* will support your personal awareness of your beliefs and practices while building understanding of your educational ecosystem as a whole. The *Pause and Process* sections in Part II will help you define your collective context. In Part III, the *Pause and Process* sections will help you begin thinking about your collective purpose. The appendix includes implementation exercises to help you go even further in your application.

This book is for anyone working in education, working in partnerships with schools, supporting children and families, and organizing to increase educational justice in schools and districts. The classrooms that teachers lead are ecosystems. Teachers can use this book to deepen their understanding of how their classroom culture, pedagogical practices, the individual worlds of their students and families, as well as their backgrounds contribute to the classroom as a whole. Principals can engage their schools in planning. This book will help superintendents to better support each school in their district as an individual ecosystem as well as to ensure the interactions between schools, between departments, and between the central office and every school work to build and reinforce beliefs, policies, practices, and content that can generate emancipatory educational ecosystems. It will also assist superintendents in situating their district within the ecosystem of the municipality and state where they are located to better marshal the assets and resources of the ecosystem to support the district. Community organizers might use the book as an advocacy and organizing tool while philanthropy and other external organizations or agencies will find the book helpful in situating themselves in relationship to schools and school districts and partnering better with them.

This book is not a guide or an instructional manual but a call to take seriously the significance of beliefs and culture in your work as an educator. It is my intent to propel you to examine the individual and systemic beliefs operating in your educational ecosystems and to unseat deficit beliefs, systems, policies, and practices that steal belonging, purpose, pride, and excitement from Black students. In so doing, I urge you and your educational ecosystem to take responsibility for building the capacity you need to move toward emancipatory educational ecosystems where affirming beliefs and CREST guide your work.

Finally, I hope that if and when you encounter resistance when interacting with ideas, concepts, or examples that challenge you, you will choose to work with any discomfort that arises and explore what your resistance may be communicating to you.

PART I

Collective Planning

The chapters in this section provide a glimpse of the personal and professional context in which the ideas, theories, and frameworks I provide developed, introduce the concept of emancipatory educational ecosystems where affirming beliefs and culturally responsive-sustaining educational transformation (CREST) drive learning, and share conscious collectivism as a framework for the ongoing intentional partnership with stakeholders.

CHAPTER 1

We Need New Educational Paradigm

Here's Why

Just as DNA is the code of instructions for cell development, caste is the operating system for economic, political, and social interaction in the United States from the time of its gestation.

—Isabelle Wilkerson

Education is not the antecedent of failing schools, poverty, homelessness, police brutality and/or crime. Racism is; racism that is built on centuries of ideas that seek to confuse and manipulate we who are dark into never mattering to one another in this country.

—Bettina Love

As I walked through the cafeteria one day during my first year of teaching, the smell of garbage drew my attention. The cafeteria buzzed with the conversations, laughter, and movements that are uniquely the language of adolescents. The lunch line was long and slow moving. Students ate their lunch in groups, some alone, at unimpressive rectangular folding lunch tables that could have been the same tables found in my high school cafeteria. By all measures, it was an ordinary lunch period. I think the ordinariness of the scene is what made the stink of unfinished lunches, sour milk, and orange peels so prominent for me in that moment and so etched in my memory to this day. My eyes tracked the scent to the cafeteria wall where garbage bags from the two earlier lunch periods were lined up in rows festering while this group of students ate their lunch. I looked from the garbage bags to the students and stopped in my tracks, thinking, "How is it okay for children to eat their lunch in school surrounded by this trash and its foul smell?" I was enraged.

This was no ordinary lunch period. Of course, when I raised the issue with an administrator, the volume of students and capacity of the staff to remove the garbage quickly enough between periods were identified as the reason for this neglect. I knew then, as do those of you reading this now, that this seemingly unharmful environmental nuisance would not be allowed to happen just anywhere. It happened in this cafeteria on this day forty-six years after *Brown v. Board of Education* because the school and the students it served met the criteria necessary to normalize the neglectful and dehumanizing presence of garbage during a high school lunch period. You could check the boxes:

- Urban ✓
- Majority Black and brown students ✓
- Immigrant students ✓
- Students who speak a first language other than English ✓
- Students living below the poverty threshold ✓

When I walked out of the cafeteria, I saw a few of my students. They smiled or waved. I waved back at them. Sometimes I would go sit and eat with them, joining in their lunchtime shenanigans. On this day, I kept it moving, too angry to sit with them without drawing them into a discussion about what I had observed. Lunch was their time to be free and unencumbered. I did not have the right to take that from them. At the start of a period later that day, I did ask a class for their thoughts about what I had seen. They responded, "We didn't even notice, Miss."

MY DISCONTENT

My call to teach was driven by a nascent awareness of how public education affects Black students. I do believe, however, this single observation in a high school cafeteria made the invisible dehumanization of Black students coursing through the education system visible to me in new ways through a heightened sensory experience that may have continued to seem ordinary to others. This incident, while specific to my experience on a particular day and time at High Point High School, where I taught, is in no way an isolated occurrence—not by any stretch of the imagination.

High Point was an overcrowded school with 4,000 students and a ten-period day that cycled the students through the building so that by lunchtime, it was at its highest capacity. Students were not assigned lockers and went from class to class the entire day carrying everything they came to school with, including coats, bookbags, books, school supplies, and instruments. In some cases, students were not allowed to take textbooks home. When they arrived in the morning, some before the first period began at 7:15, the students waited, rain or shine, in the winter and the summer, in a long line outside the school to go through the metal detectors. Because teachers were not assigned classrooms, I pushed a cart piled with books and anything else I might need from classroom to classroom five times a day, sometimes having to use the elevator to get to a class on another floor. I was notorious for forgetting the chalk because my mind just could not grasp the fact that you took the chalk with you when you left one classroom to go to the next. (I mean, seriously, who had time to think about that?) Teachers were required to lock their doors to keep the students who chose the hallways instead of their classes from entering their classrooms while we were teaching. Rarely do I recall seeing teachers at their classroom door in between periods, and I have fewer recollections of seeing them or the principal in the hallways during the school day. School safety officers and the sound of walkie-talkies were omnipresent throughout the building. I remember being thoroughly amazed and bewildered to see handcuffs hanging from school safety officers' belt loops.

This school was not organized for learning. Please don't get me wrong. Learning *did* happen here, and there were administrators, teachers, and students who worked extremely hard to make sure that it did. I learned and benefitted so much from mentoring from teachers like Jaime Johnson, Amy White, Derrick Davidson, and Sophia Johns; was supported by my vice principal Scott Walker; and grew tremendously with Amy Ortiz, who was also a first-year teacher. They coached me through lesson planning, navigating the school, building relationships with parents and guardians, and creating a classroom environment that hovered above the conditions of the school. Observing their classes, I soaked up as much as possible and wanted to be like them. I saw artful teaching from these teachers in classes where care, kindness, expectations, and joy were palpable in rich discussions, spontaneous laughter, and meaningful feedback. Their classes—inviting, rhythmic, and fluid—were nothing like the general atmosphere of the school. They were worlds of their own, oases in the building. I have always wondered what they would have been like in a school designed for them to exist. You see, these classes were anomalies. They were the "bright-spots" within an otherwise struggling ecosystem. While these teachers managed to transform their classes into healthy learning environments, they did so while compensating for the dysfunction around them. The positive feedback loop from the school to these classrooms was minimal. These talented teachers were required to be more resourceful, adaptive, and creative to nurture and maintain the positive learning experiences they created with their students. Many say this resourcefulness, ability to adapt, and creativity make those working in under-resourced schools and districts better educators. And, while I agree with the sentiment, I still do not think the conditions or the exertion they demanded are healthy. Nor do I think it is any more sustainable for these classes or other classes like them to function well in a toxic school environment than I think it is realistic to expect roses to grow from concrete. I did not exit the cafeteria that afternoon saying, "The garbage bags in this cafeteria are evidence that this school is a toxic ecosystem." I was certain that discarding bags of refuse where children eat was acceptable only because these students were Black and brown children from a disenfranchised urban neighborhood. But, at this point in my career, I had no way of articulating how the systems, practices, behaviors, and beliefs evident in this school were intentionally working to produce an ecosystem, healthy or not.

In schools across this nation, some Black students eat lunch in cafeterias that reek of trash. They sit in classrooms that are either too hot or too cold, where all kinds of vermin roam, and engage in lessons from textbooks that either completely exclude the contributions of the groups to which they belong or essentialize them into racist stereotypes or demeaning tropes. Black students are disproportionately referred for special education and suspended and expelled from school. They are taught by teachers who, having learned from the same textbooks, may implicitly believe their students will make little to no contribution to the world, in schools that are disconnected from the families and communities they serve and that function as a microcosm of the racial oppression, disparities, and inequities that exist in the larger social reality surrounding them. Education scholar Bettina Love calls this the "educational survival complex," in which students are left learning to "merely survive in schools that mimic and reproduce the same inherently inequitable and oppressive structures of the larger society" (Love, 2019). The "educational survival complex" is a hostile and malignant ecosystem where Black students are continuously exposed to diminishing environments, messages, and learning experiences.

In 2018 I attended the Carnegie Summit on Improvement in Education with several colleagues from Newark, New Jersey. The group included administrators from Newark Public Schools (NPS) and researchers from the John C. Cornwall Center for Metropolitan Studies at Rutgers University-Newark. During one of the conference breaks, we had a casual meeting with Louis Gomez and heard more about the continuous improvement research in education. What stood out for me from the continuous improvement literature before this meeting but was amplified by the cogency of Dr. Gomez's reflection during our meeting is the idea that "Every system is perfectly designed to get the results it gets."

We can look to any number of systems for evidence of this and are likely to find it, and the idea seems to make perfectly good common sense. However, when it comes to education and other social institutions serving the public good, the prevailing paradigms generally suggest something entirely different. In the case of public education, the idea that it is the "great equalizer" shapes the metanarratives and stories about education. If education is a novel, the great equalizer is the controlling idea, the undercurrent of every policy, program, decision, partnership, and strategy implemented. As a result, public education is largely approached as if the preponderance of inequity and injustice proliferating within our schools and classrooms are not the intended outcome of our education systems but merely by-products of their flaws and inefficiencies—or, more perniciously, the deficits of Black children and their families. Nothing could be further from the truth. If you are unfamiliar with the historical foundations of schooling, a vast body of literature explicates the foundational purposes and inherently unequal design of education (Au, 2023; DeMarrais & LeCompte, 1998; Grande, 2015; Love, 2019; Perry et al., 2003; Spring, 2018; Valenzuela, 1999).

DEFINING ECOSYSTEM

So, what is an *ecosystem*? An ecosystem includes all of the living things (cells, humans, plants, animals, and organisms) in a given area, interacting with each other and also with their non-living environments (weather, earth, sun, soil, climate, and atmosphere). Ecosystems demonstrate the relationship of the whole to the parts and the ways in which the parts interact, communicate, negotiate, cooperate, and collaborate with each other to ensure the healthy functioning of the whole. Ecosystems represent the connectedness of the small to the large, the invisible to the visible. Ecosystems exist within ecosystems.

Let's start with something likely familiar to us all, say a park. The park closest to me is Branch Brook Park. Dating back to the late 1800s, it is the oldest county park in the nation and was designed by the Olmsted brothers. I love and enjoy this park. Whenever I am driving home from work or an errand, I opt to drive through the park. There are two lakes in the park, a stream for which the park is named, sprawling greenways, a dog park, tennis courts named for Althea Gibson, two baseball fields, and work-out stations in various places. It is inhabited by geese (lots of them), deer that wander about, groundhogs, rabbits, field mice, insects of all kinds, birds, neighborhood cats, and I'm sure, many other species. In the spring, the largest variety and amount of cherry blossoms in the nation explode, drawing thousands of visitors to the park for festivals, wedding pictures, lunches in the grass, and religious events. Aside from being my preferred place for respite, this active, bustling park is an ecosystem composed of all the elements previously listed. Each of these plants and animals is an individual, living its own separate life. The stream that flows through the park, for instance, is its own ecosystem home to countless species, including fish, insects, and algae. Each baseball field is also an independent ecosystem that includes the field, the trees, and players and spectators. But all of the plants, animals, and spaces are also part of a larger ecosystem—Branch Brook Park.

CLASSROOMS, SCHOOLS, AND DISTRICTS ARE RACIALIZED ECOSYSTEMS

Every aspect of a school affects the other parts as well as the entire school. First and foremost, schools are physical locations where people enter complex interactions with each other and assume various functions to contribute to the whole. Schools are made up of distinct physical spaces, such as classrooms, libraries, gymnasiums, offices, and of course, cafeterias. There are norms and systems that regulate how the parts relate to the whole and the messages the whole sends to the parts. The educational survival complex is the larger educational ecosystem in which our classrooms, schools, and districts are nested.

Imagine for a moment two geographic information systems (GIS) maps. One map identifies high-performing schools across a state—New Jersey, for example. The other locates the state's low-performing schools. The first map would demonstrate that in zip codes with predominantly white, high-income communities, there are no low-performing schools and that some high-performing schools exist in zip codes with majority Black low-income communities. The second map would show that in zip codes with majority Black low-income communities, the majority of schools are low-performing and some zip codes with majority Black low-income communities have no high-performing schools. If school performance is held as the constant by zip code, what would be revealed in these maps are patterns of race and socioeconomic status that hold tightly to broader trends in social inequality, and we might reasonably conclude, these patterns influence distribution of resources and opportunity in schools. Of course, there are outliers. For example, there are high-performing schools in majority Black low-income communities just as I describe above there are "bright spots" in otherwise struggling schools.

The *Equality of Opportunity Report*, released in 1966 by James Coleman and colleagues, demonstrated that schools have little effect on students' academic achievement outside of their family background, neighborhood context, and peer influence. The Coleman report did establish a relationship between social context and student outcomes (Coleman et al., 1966). However, because identifying the root causes of the out-of-school factors it examined was beyond the scope of the report and perhaps outside even the scientific thinking of the time, the Coleman report, while highlighting the significance of social context, reinforced racist and deficit views of Black students and poor communities. More policies, programs, and research that attempted to "fix" Black families and children and not strategies to dismantle the structural and institutional racism that creates the ecosystems in which Black children live and go to school resulted from the Coleman report.

The idea that strong schools build strong communities is another view that links schools and communities to galvanize broad support for educational reform efforts. In a paper written a decade ago, my colleague Pedro Noguera and I made a similar argument about a transformation initiative taking place in Newark Public Schools at that time called The Broader Bolder Approach to Education (BBA). In this paper, we stated, "Rather than wait for a transformation of the local economy, the BBA strategy is based on the theory that it may be possible to spur economic development and improve the quality of life for a greater number of residents by transforming the schools. Though this proposition has never been tested at such a large scale before, the theory behind BBA is based on the recognition that education is both a cause of many of the problems that plague the city and a potential solution to those problems" (Noguera & Wells, 2011). I now recognize there are at least two major oversights to this argument. First, education is a primary vehicle for the propagation of economic and social inequality—and intentionally so. Second, education can only be a solution to any of our social problems to the extent that it is purposefully designed to produce entirely different social outcomes.

The fact of the matter is that in no era of history since the transatlantic slave trade began has the American ecosystem been designed for Black people to thrive. From legal enslavement to Jim Crow to the New Jim Crow, we have, by and large, endured physical and psychological aggression, toxicity, danger, and violence (Solorzano & Huber-Perez, 2020). Transforming education requires setting out to deliberately eliminate these conditions in schools and school districts. If we are to eliminate the aggression, toxicity, danger, and violence that Black students routinely experience in school, we must first acknowledge schools are doing a pretty good job at what they were designed to do—maintain Black people as a permanent underclass in American society (Wilkerson, 2021). Second, we must make a moral decision to reject deficit beliefs like white supremacy and anti-Blackness and the racial inequality they create. Finally, we must challenge and abolish anti-Blackness wherever it appears in our work as educators and replace it with beliefs and methods that affirm and uplift Black students.

Before continuing, it is important that we have a shared understanding of what I mean when white supremacy and anti-Blackness are used in this book. There are many definitions and explanations for both beliefs. The following statements draw from existing definitions to describe white supremancy and anti-Blackness and how they work systemically.

"White supremacy is 'the all-encompassing centrality and assumed superiority of people defined and perceived as white, and the practices based upon that assumption (DiAngelo, 2017)." It "assigns values to real or imagined differences in order to justify the perceived inherent superiority of whites over People of Color that defines the right and power of whites to dominance" (Solorzano, Perez, & Huber, 2020) and operates as a "global system that confers unearned power and privilege on those who become identified as white while conferring disprivilege and disempowerment on those who become identified as People of Color" (Allen, 2001).

Anti-Blackness is the beliefs, attitudes, practices, and behaviors that create the specific forms of racism that systematically marginalize, dehumanize, denigrate, and disempower Black people (Comrie et al., n.d.). Anti-Blackness positions Black people as inherently inferior and codifies a continuum of social belonging on which all people, including all people of color, are situated but on which Black people are categorically denied the benefits of membership. Anti-Blackness is the ideological, structural, and cultural foundation on which the violence; lack of access to education, jobs, and healthcare; psychological abuse; exposure to toxic, unhealthful environments; and disenfranchisement we experience are normalized. Anti-Blackness exists and operates both at the individual and structural level within our educational ecosystems and generates learning opportunities that perpetuate the mistreatment and erasure of Black people in schools and society.

Table 1.1 provides definitions for terms that describe commonly held beliefs that perpetuate the educational survival complex, including abbreviated definitions for white supremacy and anti-Blackness. In this book, I discuss these terms as deficit beliefs because they work individually and collectively in our schools to locate deficits in Black people and consciously and unconsciously shape the learning opportunities and experiences afforded to Black students.

TABLE 1.1 • Definitions of Deficit Beliefs

BELIEF	DEFINITION
White Supremacy	White supremacy is "the assigning of values to real or imagined differences in order to justify the perceived inherent superiority of whites over People of Color that defines the right and power of whites to dominance" (Solorzano & Perez, Huber, 2020).
Anti-Blackness	Anti-Blackness is the beliefs, attitudes, practices, and behaviors that create the specific forms of racism that systematically marginalize, dehumanize, denigrate, and disempower Black people.
Meritocracy	Meritocracy is the belief that people are rewarded, successful, or afforded privileges, opportunities, or status based on the talent, abilities, and efforts they demonstrate.
Competition	Competition is the belief that there are not enough resources to go around and domination demonstrates strength, character, and rights.
Individualism	Individualism is the belief that people should be independent and self-reliant and that individual interests, needs, and actions are a priority.

EMANCIPATORY EDUCATIONAL ECOSYSTEMS

Districts and schools serving predominantly Black students and communities have been saddled for far too long with solving the problems created by structural racism and social inequality. Education is, on the one hand, viewed as the vaccine to almost every one of our social problems while, on the other, it is scapegoated for the intractability of poverty, unemployment, and other issues in Black communities. This book challenges both views as it sets out to be explicit about the role of white supremacy and anti-Blackness in our classrooms, schools, and districts so that we can strive to create emancipatory educational ecosystems where Black students have learning experiences that "create in a person the ability to look at the world for (them)self, to make (their) own decisions," and "act to liberate themselves, and the world, from injustice" (Baldwin, 1963; Freire, 2010). Emancipatory educational ecosystems are governed by beliefs that affirm Black children and immerse them in learning where their identities and cultures matter.

Emancipatory educational ecosystems is a conceptual intervention that "has great potential to undo deficit constructions of (Black students) and their (learning)" (Haddix & Ruiz, 2012). The fact that my students "didn't even notice" the presence or smell of garbage in the cafeteria during their lunch reveals just how normalized degraded and dehumanized learning environments can be for Black students and for educators. Educators fail to respond to these and other deplorable conditions or acts of mistreatment because of deficit beliefs. As a result, our personal and systemic belief systems must be vigorously investigated so that the specific ways deficit beliefs manifest in us and in our educational ecosystems can be confronted and disrupted.

I suspect, given the demographics of education scholars and professionals, being confronted with the idea that schools are institutions designed to normalize white supremacy and perpetuate racial inequality is cognitively disconcerting for some. We are, after all, taught to believe in the promise of education as the pathway to equality and opportunity for all. For others, myself included, the first encounter with the historical facts, artifacts, and policies that gave rise to what we now know as public education was a major "aha" moment. It brought my experiences as both a student and a teacher in public schools into sharper focus and provided a lens for me to better understand them. It may be discomforting and cause physical and emotional stress to see our world, our neighborhoods, and our schools as ecosystems designed to degrade the humanity of entire groups of people or grapple with our participation. Nevertheless, if education is ever to be an instrument of freedom or even equity, it is essential that we do and, in so doing, reconcile our personal histories and roles in the ecosystems to which we belong.

Treating our classrooms, schools, and districts as educational ecosystems can help us recognize the interrelationship between the aspects of schooling we can visibly observe (for example, neighborhoods, buildings, classrooms, cafeterias, curricula and textbooks, relationships between people, budgets, etc.) and the beliefs that underlie what is visible to us. This paradigm shift also gives us an opportunity to explicate new beliefs and practices for organizing how the different aspects of education interact; generating relationships between schools, districts, and the communities where they are situated; and designing learning so we can collectively move toward emancipatory educational ecosystems.

RIPPLES IN THE FIELD: FROM PERSONAL TO UNIVERSAL

I have witnessed and experienced firsthand how activated and engaged ecosystems can catalyze educational transformation through my work in Newark, New Jersey, over the last fifteen years. When people come together to define and understand their shared problems, to excavate and examine their beliefs and values, and to set a course to a new vision of what is possible, they experience the interdependency that exists among all living beings and the environments in which they interact. People acting collectively invariably awaken and harness their power to influence and shape the world around them, including the interplay of the policies, practices, strategies, and institutions impacting public education. In this book, I draw on reflections of my own experiences as a teacher and a student, data collected in a district I call Hilltop, and efforts in Newark, New Jersey, to contextualize my ideas about emancipatory educational ecosystems.

As a Black woman educator, organizer, and researcher, I am purposefully, intentionally, focused on the learning environments where Black children are educated. The conceptual and methodological contributions I make in this book about educating Black students have developed at the intersections of my professional work, my intellectual curiosity, my commitment to personal and social transformation, and my lived experiences as a Black woman. The subjectivity and positionality of my life and work matter to my work, as does yours. I do this work because of who I am and what I have experienced in my life because of who I am. I present the ideas in this book to encourage the awareness that we do our work as educators as racialized individuals who have been influenced by our families, communities, and the ideologies, systems, and institutions with which we interact. The work we do is complex and full of contradictions, and those of us who do it are a part of the mess. As Rumi says, "The wound is the place where light enters." And so, as I have been reflective about my own experiences and beliefs while becoming a teacher, an educator, and a catalyst for educational transformation, I could not help but think about how beliefs, systems, and experiences influence what we all do individually and collectively and ultimately shape what we seek to achieve. While these inquiries may seem too challenging or defeatist to some, I propose that it is precisely these reflective practices that strengthen our capacity to imagine the spaces that center the identities, cultures, histories, experiences, and aspirations of Black students in their learning.

As an undergraduate English major at Temple University, I read *Playing in the Dark: Whiteness and the Literary Imagination* by Toni Morrison. I continue to read and reference this book frequently. In the preface, T. Morrison (1998) suggests,

> Living in a nation of people who *decided* that their worldview would combine agendas for individual freedom and mechanisms for devastating racial oppression presents a singular landscape for a writer.

We who educate Black students must also travail the reality of this landscape in our work. We must do it with the moral conviction and will to abolish anything that seeks to diminish the embers of genius, pride, creativity, power, and wonder Black students bring with them to our schools and classrooms. We must have the individual and collective agency to acquire the beliefs and knowledge needed to create emancipatory educational ecosystems where Black students experience belonging, purpose, pride, and joy for learning. This book unapologetically calls you to do this. I now turn to examples of efforts to transform education in Newark, New Jersey, that contribute to my belief that affirming beliefs and capacity for culturally responsive-sustaining education transformation (CRSET) are needed to create learning that elicits the genius of Black students.

Additional Resources

Love, B. (2019). *We want to do more than survive: Abolitionist teaching and the pursuit of educational freedom*. Beacon.

Ruiz, O. I., & Sealey-Ruiz, Y. (2022). Our journey toward racial literacy: A mother and daughter's story. *Journal of Adolescent & Adult Literacy, 66*(3), 199–202. https://doi.org/10.1002/jaal.1272

CHAPTER 2

Disrupting the Norm

Central High School and the Newark Global Village School Zone

When you take on this huge organization, you don't have a magic wand, and you cannot pretend that you do.

—Marion Bolden

Few people understand what to do once the door is open and the power structure says, "Come on in and sit down at the table."

—Junius Williams

The first period of my very first day teaching at High Point, two students, Mark and Denise, were present for class. Thirty-four students were listed on my roster. As I sat with those two students and circled the little bubbles next to their names, I was nervous but determined. Like every first-year teacher, I had no idea what to expect. Unlike many educators who will read this book, I had no formal teacher preparation. I had been granted a provisional teaching certificate that allowed me two years to complete the education courses required to obtain a full certificate. I had not been inside a public school classroom since I had graduated from high school ten years earlier. At my first departmental meeting, I received a lesson planning template, various policies and memos, and a grade book from my vice principal. After the meeting, a veteran teacher took me to the book room to select the books for my classes. I chose *Romeo and Juliet*, *Of Mice and Men*, and *Night* because I read them as a student. Though I had not yet read it, I also chose *The House on Mango Street* because the setting seemed relevant and because I knew many of my students would be Latino/a. On the first day of school, when Mark and Denise filled two of the forty empty desks in my classroom, I knew absolutely nothing. Nothing, except that they were there and that mattered to me.

So how did an inexperienced and uncertified teacher like me end up at High Point? After completing the paperwork required to obtain a provisional certificate from the High Point Board of Education, I was given a list of schools where I could interview for a position. I interviewed at three schools. The first interview was at a job fair held by the district. The principal who interviewed me for this school told me I had obvious passion but no philosophy of teaching and wished me luck. My second interview was held in a trailer where a newly formed school had recently been established and was looking for teachers as it grew. A returning teacher and the principal interviewed me. At the end of this interview, the principal praised me for my strong academic background, enthusiasm, and passion (again). She said she wished she could hire me, but her students needed teachers with more experience. Before she concluded the interview, the principal said that the school where she was previously a vice principal could use me, offered to call the vice principal on my behalf, and sent me on my way to High Point. I interviewed and was hired at High Point on the very same day.

At times, when I reflect on how I ended up at High Point, I am certain that being hired on the spot with no experience just before school started was a leading indicator that Mark, Denise, and all the other students at the school didn't matter in a larger context. It wasn't until graduate school that I became familiar with the research about how students with the greatest needs are more likely to be assigned novice teachers or, in my case, novice and provisionally certified teachers. Three other first-year provisionally certified teachers were hired by my department at the same time as I was. In a department of twelve, one-fourth of us had never taught in a classroom before, not even as student teachers. The practice of placing inexperienced teachers with students who need and deserve a higher level of instructional expertise is a sentence to debilitating and inequitable learning conditions and one example of how the "educational survival complex" makes the learning of Black students insignificant.

There are other times when I think that entering teaching with a belief in Black students and a desire to be where I was teaching was more qualifying than possessing teacher and preservice training meant to prepare me for complicity in the educational survival complex. In this book, I situate beliefs as the currents that wire our work as educators. Our beliefs about our students are transmitted to them through the relationships we develop with them, the content and instructional practices we use, and our efforts to meet them where they are (Jackson, 2010). Believing in my students compelled me to care about what was happening in our classroom and to fill as many of my gaps as I could on my own. So while I did not formally have any training in theories of learning, classroom management strategies, lesson design, or creating learning assessments, culturally responsive or otherwise, the belief that my students mattered led me to use the impactful strategies I could remember from my learning experience and seek all the resources I could to help me make my classroom as meaningful as possible for my students.

My work over the last twenty years has taught me that it is true that both beliefs and expertise are necessary but insufficient by themselves. The belief in Black students and their communities is nonnegotiable. In Chapter 8, I introduce beliefs that affirm and value Black people in general and Black students in particular. But without the training and systems that support a belief system that affirms Black students, our ability to transform our beliefs about what students can achieve into learning that elicits their "high intellectual performance" is limited. Culturally responsive-sustaining education transformation (CRSET), which I discuss in Chapter 9, is so important because it provides the methods through which affirming beliefs become policy, systems, and practice. However, training and professional development without an affirming belief system cannot be responsibly or appropriately put into practice.

Since 2006, I have worked as part of the educational ecosystem in Newark, New Jersey, and I have also collaborated with schools and districts in various parts of the country. In 2006, I became the project coordinator of the New Jersey Education Organizing Coalition (NJEOC), a cross-city advocacy coalition formed to galvanize support to maintain equitable funding under *Abbott v. Burke*. In 2009, I joined Pedro Noguera at the Metropolitan Center for Urban Education at New York University as the director of the Broader Bolder Approach to Education (BBA), where I collaborated with seven principals from the Newark Public Schools (NPS) to design and implement a major school reform initiative called the Newark Global Village School Zone (NGVSZ). When Ras Baraka, one of the principals with whom I worked in the NGVSZ, was elected mayor of Newark in 2014, I was appointed chief education officer for the City of Newark and worked in partnership with educators, community leaders, and students to have local control returned to the Newark Board of Education (NBOE) as well as to build support across the city for community schools. After local control was returned to the NBOE in 2018, I, along with a team of scholars and educators, worked with NPS to develop a ten-year strategic plan called, "The Next Decade: 2020–2030 Strategic Plan."

The examples I share in this chapter are various educational efforts in Newark with which I have been involved over the last decade. These initiatives have, over time, contributed to a widely held ecological view of education in Newark. I share these examples not to put forward ideas of how to achieve perfect educational transformation. None of my examples are perfect, nor did they coalesce seamlessly into an ecological view. The flaws and limitations of my examples are, in one way or another, indicative of the powerful influence that dominant beliefs about race, culture, and learning exert on the education of all students, especially Black students. I offer these examples, and particularly those of the NGVSZ, to illustrate that despite the recalcitrance of the educational survival complex, affirming beliefs and CRSET can give us the power, knowledge, and resources to loosen their grip on the spirits and minds of Black students. I focus on these efforts, which unfolded over a ten-year period in Newark collectively because I think it is important to provide a window into the cumulative impacts of sustained commitment and focus so that others might resist the siren songs of silver bullets and superheroes and take the long view.

A BROADER BOLDER APPROACH TO EDUCATION

The Broader Bolder Approach to Education (BBA) was launched in Newark in 2009 following a keynote address Pedro Noguera delivered to a diverse audience of advocates, policymakers, practitioners, and government officials at a statewide dropout prevention conference held in Trenton, New Jersey. BBA is a national policy and advocacy campaign established by education experts and advocates, including Dr. Noguera, that "advances evidence-based strategies to mitigate the impacts of poverty-related disadvantages on teaching and learning" (Broader Bolder Approach to Education [BBA], 2022). BBA links school improvement efforts to broader community development and pays attention to academic skills and knowledge, as well as to the well-being and development of the whole child. The BBA model calls for the development of preK–12 educational initiatives that are developed according to five principles:

1. Continued school improvement efforts
2. Increased investment in high-quality early childhood, preschool, and kindergarten education
3. Increased investment in health services
4. Improved quality for out-of-school time programs
5. Community and economic development

BBA initiatives have been established across the country to create knowledge for professional training and student learning that informs ongoing school improvement efforts. For example, local BBA initiatives develop long-term partnerships between a local university and schools to foster ongoing professional development for teachers in subject matter content areas and pedagogy, create alignment between the school curriculum and local industry, and develop leadership among parents and students on issues related to school performance and community development.

Dr. Noguera's remarks at the conference highlighted BBA and drew the attention of New Jersey governor Jon Corzine, who urged him to bring the BBA approach to New Jersey. After discussions with the newly appointed state superintendent of the Newark Public Schools (NPS), Dr. Clifford Janey, it was agreed that BBA would be piloted in NPS.

A SNAPSHOT OF NEWARK PUBLIC SCHOOLS

Located in the Mid-Atlantic region, New Jersey is one of the wealthiest states in the nation. It is also one of the nation's most residentially segregated states. Across the state, some cities and townships appear to be diverse, but within them, there are patterns of hypersegregation. Segregation within segregation is the typical social topology of New Jersey's communities and schools. The racial segregation in New Jersey, like elsewhere, is not benign but is accompanied by significant income and wealth disparities. In Hohokus, the wealthiest zip code in New Jersey, residents are 92 percent white and the average income was $284,946 in 2019 (United States Zip Codes, 2023.) During the same year, the average income in Camden, the predominantly Black (35 percent) and Latino/a (36 percent) and poorest zip code in the state, was $28,623 (Data USA, 2023).

Newark, New Jersey, is the third oldest city in the nation and the largest city and school district in New Jersey. As a major commuter hub along the Northeast Corridor, Newark intersects with and is adjacent to three major highways and, in 2019, 46,336,452 passengers flew in and out of Newark Liberty Airport. The Newark Port is the largest on the East Coast and the second largest in the country, making Newark a vital commercial asset to the region and nation. Newark is 48 percent Black and 36 percent Latino. Black people have been the majority of the city's residents since the 1960s. Over 30 percent of Newark's residents are foreign-born. Approximately 46.3 percent of Newark residents speak a first language other than English. In 2019, the average income of Newarkers was $37,476 (Data USA, 2023). Despite the wealth that flows through and around Newark, it is consistently among the top ten poorest cities in the state (Stacker, 2022).

Newark manifests residential segregation among racial and ethnic groups and according to income. These patterns are mirrored in the city's schools, contributing to student populations that are hypersegregated, particularly by race and ethnicity. These and other socioeconomic dynamics have shaped how the educational survival complex influences educational ecosystems in Newark. Since the 1990s, there have been three major influences on public education in Newark. First, the landmark New Jersey Supreme Court ruling in *Abbott v. Burke* sought to mitigate funding inequities and establish criteria for school reform, including providing high-quality preschool for all three- and four-year-olds in districts that received *Abbott* funds. In 1995, the New Jersey Department of Education assumed state control of the Newark Board of Education, four years after setting a national precedent in 1991 when the state took control of the Paterson Public Schools. State intervention is another example of the force the education survival complex exerts primarily in predominantly Black school districts (Morel, 2018). Following the passage of the New Jersey Charter Schools Act in 1995, charter schools began operating in Newark. For twenty-two years, the state takeover of the Newark Public Schools was the primary instrument for educational reform of NPS. Culminating with the last two state-appointed superintendents, state control of NPS drew increasingly upon reform strategies that closed neighborhood schools, narrowed curriculum, eliminated departments, programs, and student supports, and contributed to the growth of charter schools in the city.

When the BBA initiative began in 2009, there was a pervasive narrative that Newark was a failing district and more educational survival complex reforms were needed. There was very little political support for a strategy, like BBA, that centered the community, engaged school leaders and their staff, emphasized collaboration, and desired more than higher scores on standardized tests. The prevailing view was Black students needed schools that put more emphasis on discipline, basic skill acquisition, and grit. When BBA was launched in 2009, 54 percent of the city's residents were Black (this includes immigrants from the Caribbean and Africa) and another 30 percent were Latino (the majority were Puerto Rican, but there were also large numbers of residents from the Dominican Republic, Mexico, Brazil, and Central America) (Central High School [CHS], 2010). In the Central Ward schools that were identified for the initiative, over 90 percent of students were Black (Civil Rights Data Collection, n.d.). The few signs of economic development or improvement to the city's housing market and infrastructure and few new hotels, sporting arenas, or cultural centers were limited to the downtown area where few of the Central Ward families and students lived.

THE NEWARK GLOBAL VILLAGE SCHOOL ZONE

One high school and six elementary schools in Newark's Central Ward were identified for the BBA initiative: Central High School, 18th Avenue Elementary School, Cleveland Elementary School, Newton Street Elementary School, Quitman Street Community School, Burnet Street Elementary School, and Sussex Avenue Elementary School. This feeder pattern was selected by Superintendent Janey because it enrolled the smallest number of students: 3,500. Most of the students attending these schools were Black, including first-generation Haitian and African immigrant students as well as Black students whose families had resided in Newark for generations (CHS, 2010).

As is often the with new initiatives, the schools did not volunteer to participate. The seven principals leading the schools received a call during summer break informing them that the partnership had been formed and their schools would be participating. Many of the principals had previously heard Dr. Noguera speak or read his books, so while they expressed some of the reticence that accompanies top-down reform, they also greeted BBA as a unique opportunity. I worked directly with the principals to design the Newark BBA. Together with their school communities, the seven BBA principals developed their collective vision for BBA based on the context of their schools and renamed the initiative *The Newark Global Village School Zone*. Our goal was to transform these seven schools so that they were able to work together to support the academic progress of the students they shared by connecting to families and the community. This included the alignment of school improvement with efforts to address their social and developmental needs and connecting community resources and assets. We worked from the theory of change that engaging Newark's educational ecosystem from the top-down, bottom-up, inside-out, and outside-in simultaneously would generate the knowledge, will, and resources to support and sustain change.

From June 2009 through 2012, when Dr. Janey was replaced as the state-appointed superintendent, the schools worked individually and collaboratively in four key areas: community engagement, integrated social services, professional development, and expanded learning time. In addition to students, families, and community leaders, this work activated and empowered collaboration between external partners. For example, The Academy for Educational Development (AED, now FHI 360), Bank Street College of Education, and Children's Literacy Initiative (CLI) worked collaboratively across the schools and with NYU to align and integrate their existing efforts with the goals of the NGVSZ. In a poignant demonstration of this collective approach, all of the instructional partners working with the NGVSZ collaborated to conduct informal observations of classrooms in all seven schools to identify the common strengths and needs. A comprehensive professional development plan that supported the collective needs of all seven schools and addressed the specific needs at each school was developed. Instructional partners working collectively not only facilitated instructional alignment but also allowed resources to go further.

It is impossible to detail the scope of the planning, activities, and resources that went into the development of the NGVSZ for you here. This quote from a press release issued by parents active in the effort demonstrates the essence of the approach and the clarity of vision among stakeholders: "(NGVSZ) is responsive to the Community's call for action to promote meaningful grassroots reform wherein national best practices and community resources support a well-rounded, culturally relevant, enriched and engaging college-preparatory curriculum." The NGVSZ was developed and implemented through the collaborative efforts of school leaders, teachers, parents, educational partners, students, community organizations, and local and national foundations. The following timeline provides a glimpse of how the focus areas and the engagement of stakeholders unfolded over the initiative's duration:

- **August 2009:** BBA introduced to principals, NPS administrators, and community leaders at Central High School.
- **2009–2010 school year:** The principals began planning collaboratively.

- **November 2009:** Leadership teams from all seven NGVSZ schools participated in a learning trip to the Berkeley School to learn about the Berkeley Integrated Resource Initiative (BIRI) where they visited schools and health clinics.
- **January 2010:** First community meeting took place at Central High School.
- **Spring 2010:** The principals developed and presented a transformation plan to Dr. Janey, and the initiative is renamed the Newark Global Village School Zone.
- **June 2010:** A city-wide planning conference was held to bring NGVSZ stakeholders together to participate in planning for the NGVSZ.
- **June 2010:** Central High School was awarded a $6.8 million New Jersey Department of Education School Improvement Grant.
- **August 2010:** First NGVSZ Leadership Retreat was held with inclusive teams comprised of administrators, teachers, parents, and partners.
- **2010–2011 school year:** NGVSZ schools aligned improvement strategies, professional development activities, support services, and resources, including professional development from the Children's Literacy Initiative (CLI), Bank Street College of Education, AED, LitLife, National Urban Alliance for Excellent Schools (NUA), and Dr. Alfred Tatum.
- **October 2010:** NGVSZ received a donation from philanthropist Emily Meschter to purchase culturally relevant libraries for each school.
- **April 2011:** Leadership teams from all seven NGVSZ schools participated in a learning trip to Colorado Springs, where they visited schools and classrooms and met with Superintendent Mike Miles.
- **June 2011:** With the support of philanthropist Emily Meschter, NGVSZ provided every student in each school with three culturally relevant books for their home libraries.
- **August 2011:** Second NGVSZ Leadership Retreat was held with inclusive teams comprised of administrators, teachers, parents, and partners.
- **2011–2012 school year:** Community Engagement coordinator Carolota Tagoe held monthly "Chat and Chews" with parents, including a "Spring Training" for dads.

- **September 2011:** NGVSZ schools continued to align improvement strategies, professional development activities, support services, and resources, including professional development co-facilitated by teachers and educational support partners.
- **June 2012:** Two NGVSZ elementary schools were closed, and four became turnaround schools. The NGVSZ was disbanded.

THE SALIENCE OF BELIEFS AND KNOWLEDGE

At the center of the NGVSZ was Central High School (CHS), one of the district's five comprehensive high schools. CHS was founded in 1911. In 2008, under the leadership of principal Ras Baraka, the school moved to a new state-of-the-art facility located in the heart of the city's Central Ward neighborhoods. The new school building, including a health center, public park, and athletic facilities, was designed to be a neighborhood hub. The NGVSZ helped the school galvanize around this purpose. As you may observe from the timeline, our efforts engaged many technical aspects of school reform, including using data across a system to inform decision-making; developing curricula frameworks, benchmarks, and rubrics; implementing job-embedded collaborative professional development; and community engagement. However, with CHS as the anchor of the NGVSZ, these and other aspects of our work were guided by the culturally responsive-sustaining principles and practices of the school.

Central was led and staffed by teachers, security guards, maintenance workers, counselors, and other school staff who unambiguously believed in the brilliance of their students and, therefore, created a school culture that was designed to ignite the genius already within them. Principal Baraka, who is the son of Black Arts Movement leaders and activists Amiri and Aminah Baraka, brought not only years of educational experience to the school but also a depth of historical, cultural, and political knowledge as well. He used his upbringing in the Black Arts and Black Political movements of the seventies and college activism to inform the purposes, culture, and practices of Central. This included a very focused approach to staffing and professional development. Staff in all roles at Central had some knowledge of the impacts of racism and oppression on schools or a willingness to learn. Many attended Newark Public Schools as students. A significant portion of the staff lived in

Newark. But not all the staff were from or lived in Newark. Baraka hired staff from all backgrounds depending on their propensity to contribute to a school culture that affirmed and challenged the intellect of the Black students they educated.

As a comprehensive urban high school, Central High School was and is nested in the educational survival complex. It is part of a system locally and nationally that has reduced the education of Black children to discipline, closing the achievement gap, standardized testing, and grit. While in many schools like Central students experience daily a routine of learning that is bereft of cultural relevance or meaning to them and limited to basic skills and behavioral control, the culture at Central pushed back against these narrow confines. Culture was the heartbeat of Central. The students at Central were immersed in symbols, experiences, content, and relationships that communicated in this school they mattered. The logo on the school's blue and white uniforms, worn by students and staff alike, included four Adinkra symbols from the Akan people of Ghana that visually expressed moral lessons from proverbs, parables, and concepts (see Figure 2.1):

- Denkyem, or crocodile, is a symbol of **adaptability**.
- Aya, or fern, is a symbol of **perseverance**.
- Ananse Ntontan, or spider's web, is a symbol of **creativity**.
- Hye Won Hye, or "that which does not burn," is a symbol of **imperishability**.

FIGURE 2.1 •

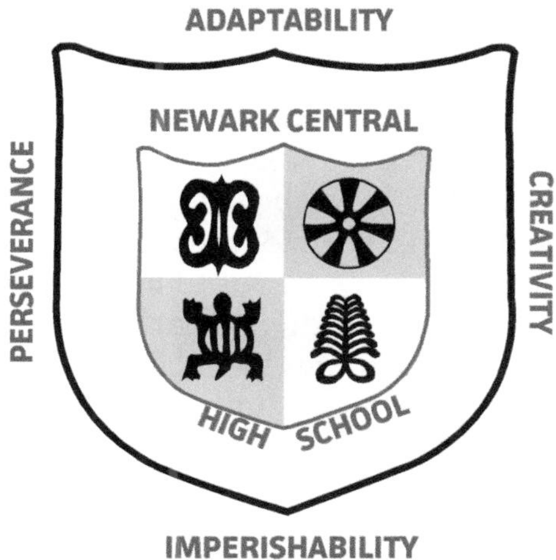

The meanings of these symbols were a part of the cultural beliefs and values of the school. Central's atrium welcomed students and visitors with inviting blue and white seating, a life-size chess board, and larger-than-life animodules students created with the Barat Foundation, a local nonprofit arts organization. An array of quotes from notable international social and political leaders including Ernesto "Che" Guevara and Trinidadian poet and political leader Aime Césaire were displayed around the perimeter of the atrium. A rendition of the painting *Aspects of Negro Life: From Slavery Through Reconstruction* by famed Harlem Renaissance artist Aaron Douglas (1934) was also prominently featured in this vibrant common space of the school. Students changed classes to the melodies of Miles Davis, Nina Simone, or John Coltrane over the intercom system and not the sound of typical bells ringing.

Relationships with and among students were another visible aspect of the school culture. The school day began with a convocation where the principal, other school staff, and student leaders brought students together to get them focused for the day. Throughout the day, staff in all positions could be regularly seen talking to students, whether moving them along to class or chatting in the cafeteria. Groups of girls were often assembled in the security office, boys in the principal's office. Advisory periods and a Student Honor Court were created. When the final class ended and students streamed out of the school to walk home, teachers, security guards, and administrators walked amongst them to ensure their safe passage. The importance of relationships extended to students' families. "I'm going to call your mother" was often heard echoing in the hallway. The community was always present in the school, whether a community organization hosting a program for students, parents meeting with the parent liaison, or community leaders visiting the school.

Classroom instruction, of course, included all the required courses, curricula, and assessments. However, not only did the school build capacity to make students' lived experiences a part of the required learning, but they also developed courses that centered culture and history. For example, as a part of the SIG grant, Central created a Social Justice Academy with a teacher-developed curriculum. Similarly, the English department began developing courses like Black Women Writers and Novel Studies. Newly arrived Haitian students took French and Haitian-Creole classes to develop proficiency in their first language that would support English language acquisition. The school expanded its advanced placement course offerings and developed a dual enrollment program with the

New Jersey Institute of Technology (NJIT) for students in its Engineering Academy.

The collective work of the NGVSZ unfolded under the influence of these cultural characteristics. Though the full implementation of the NGVSZ was cut short (as many efforts are) by changing leadership and much work remained to be completed, in just this short period of time, there were promising outcomes that suggested ongoing progress would have been achievable with our approach. For example, in May 2011, Baraka assembled Central's students and faculty into the school's auditorium to announce the school's results on the High School Proficiency Assessment (HSPA), which showed a 32.5 percent growth in English language arts (from 36.6 percent in 2010 to 69.9 percent in 2011) and a 25.9 percent growth in mathematics (from 19.9 percent in 2010 to 46 percent in 2011). The entire school community responded with pride and triumph. The graduation rate also increased from 50 percent to 80 percent in the same period. While such gains are unprecedented and to many outsiders totally unexpected, they did not surprise the principal or staff at Central who always believed in their students' potential. Many schools undertake similar technical efforts but are unable to create change. Central's early success and ongoing potential for transformation did not result solely from being data-driven or implementing evidence-based strategies. Learning for Central's students was accelerated because they were immersed in an educational ecosystem that affirmed them, viewed their culture as essential to learning, and centralized relationships. Central was striving to become an emancipatory educational ecosystem.

I am often honestly amazed at what was accomplished in such a short period of time. While I discuss Central High School as the anchor, the work and progress made were possible because it was a collective effort in which each part had a role and contributed to the whole. Working as an ecosystem with a collective purpose propelled this effort. Every person mattered. Every school mattered. Every resource mattered. The NGVSZ was abruptly dismantled, but because the work was collective, its impact did not end there.

SOUTH WARD COMMUNITY SCHOOLS INITIATIVE

In 2015, after Baraka was elected mayor of Newark, he used his bully pulpit to press then state-appointed superintendent Christopher Cerf to launch a community schools initiative.

A combination of political factors and persistent pressure from community leaders and coalitions, such as the Coalition for Effective Newark Schools, resulted in an agreement between the Mayor's Office and NPS to launch the South Ward Community Schools Initiative (SWCI). Five schools enrolling a majority of Black students were selected to participate in the initiative, which was supported from 2015 through 2019 with ten million dollars from Mark Zuckerberg's 100-million-dollar donation in 2012 and school improvement grants (SIG) awarded to the schools. The partnership plan between the City of Newark and NPS included the integrated and comprehensive elements of successful community schools but also included aspects of the reforms prioritized in the school turn-around model. Political tensions as well as the dominance of reforms endorsed by the educational survival complex challenged the effort from the outset, short-changing the ideas and voices of the students, parents, and educators who participated in their planning and undermining its impact. Nevertheless, the cooperation between the city, the school district, and community organizations empowered the community's expectations for approaches to school transformation that connect schools and communities; build partnerships to support schools, content, and instruction that engage the whole child; and collective measures of success.

THE NEXT DECADE

Local control was returned to NPS in 2018 after twenty-two years of state operation. For the first time since the district was taken over by the state in 1995, the authority to set policy and appoint the superintendent belonged to the locally elected school board. When schools opened for the 2018 through 2019 school year, the district was led by its first locally appointed superintendent in twenty-two years, Roger León. León, a locally grown leader, began his career in the district at Hawkins Street Elementary School—the same school he attended as a student—led elementary and high schools, coached the nationally acclaimed Science Park Debate Team, and was an assistant superintendent. León brought years of experience, first-hand knowledge of the neighborhoods and needs of the city, a vast network of relationships, and engagement with both the NGVSZ and the community school initiative to the role.

During his first year, León shared a vision of an educational ecosystem that supports students and families from conception to college and career and mobilized the district in a two-year strategic planning process. The logic model depicting the superintendent's vision identified all stakeholder groups, the relationships between schools and grade levels in the progression of students, the connection of institutions in the environment surrounding the district to the district and students, and various learning experiences and enrichment opportunities as parts of the new educational ecosystem (see Figure 2.2). For the first time, each part of the ecosystem could see itself in how the district was thinking about its future. Higher expectations, cultural responsiveness, increased transparency, equity, and collaboration were consistently identified as critical to the future of the district during the strategic planning process. These themes were integrated into the priorities and strategies into a ten-year strategic plan called *The Next Decade: 2020–2030 Strategic Plan* (Newark Board of Education [NBOE], 2020). But powerful learning experiences that are culturally, historically, and socially situated in Black students' lived experiences require systemically countering the educational survival complex with a belief system that affirms Black students, professional learning that builds capacity for CRSET, and internal and external accountability for addressing systemic racism.

Each of my examples encompasses an ecological view of schools and districts wherein stakeholders were able to think more holistically about the systems, policies, and practices within their ecosystem. What these examples didn't explicitly address was how beliefs operate in and through systems, nor did they set out to eradicate the deficit-beliefs that create limiting learning experiences for Black students. This is not to say that there weren't principals, teachers, parents, and partners involved who held affirming views and acted on assets-based beliefs about Black students and their communities. There were many, as Central High School demonstrates. Yet what we failed to do in these efforts was systematically expose the deficit-beliefs operating in the ecosystem and purposefully supplant them with the affirming beliefs from which an emancipatory educational ecosystem could grow. The progress Central High School made demonstrates the saliency of beliefs and culture to educating Black students. This is true whether your student population includes one Black student or one thousand Black students. I have learned from these examples that significant or sustainable change is limited without what I call *conscious collectivism*. Conscious collectivism is a framework for collectively engaging stakeholders to design emancipatory educational ecosystems. There are three components to my approach to conscious collectivism: collective planning, collective context, and collective purpose. In Chapter 3, I provide a framework for conscious collectivism.

FIGURE 2.2 ●

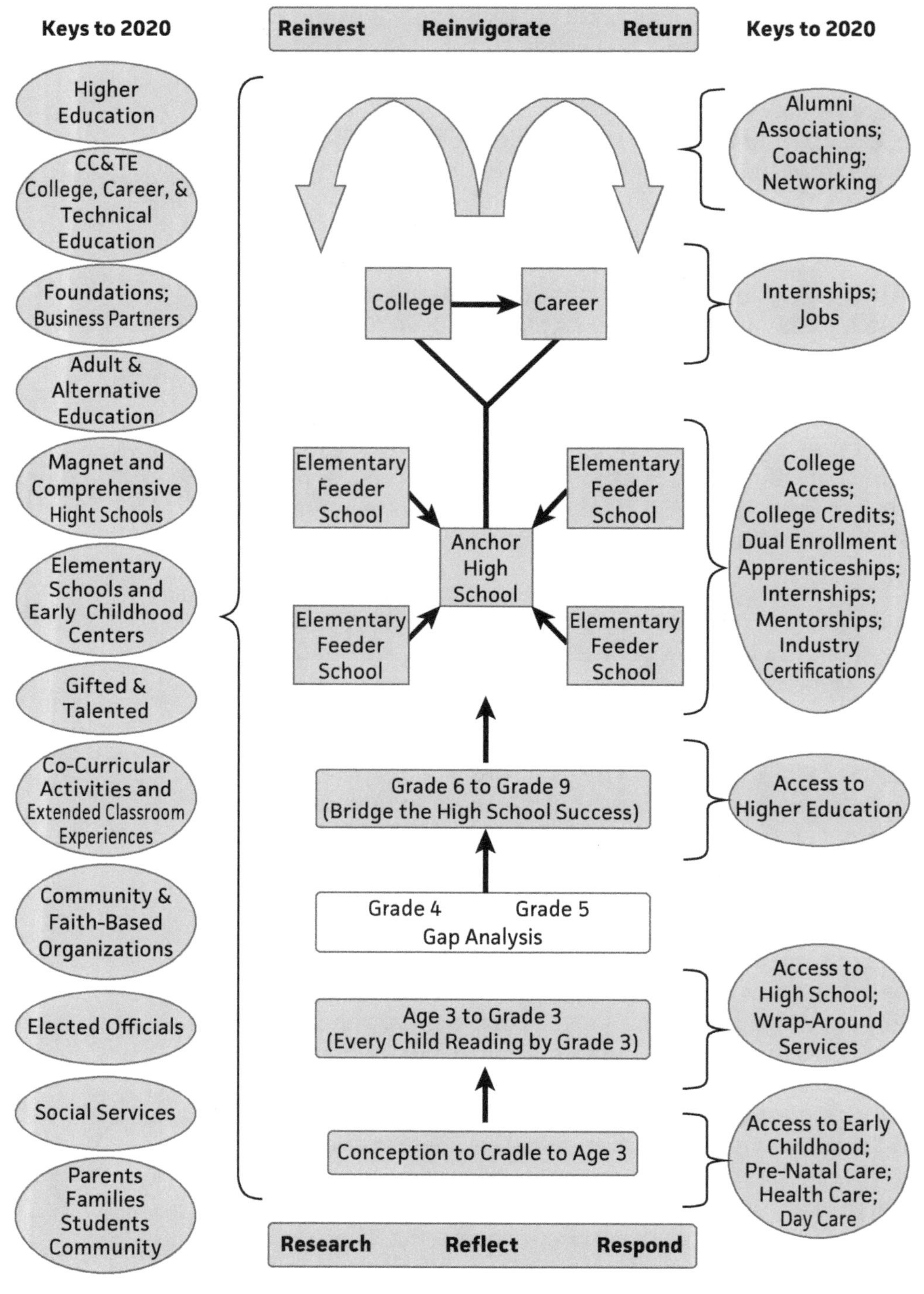
NPS CLARITY 2020
Keys to 2020
Reinvest Reinvigorate Return
Keys to 2020
Higher Education
CC&TE College, Career, & Technical Education
Foundations; Business Partners
Adult & Alternative Education
Magnet and Comprehensive Hight Schools
Elementary Schools and Early Childhood Centers
Gifted & Talented
Co-Curricular Activities and Extended Classroom Experiences
Community & Faith-Based Organizations
Elected Officials
Social Services
Parents Families Students Community
College
Career
Elementary Feeder School
Elementary Feeder School
Anchor High School
Elementary Feeder School
Elementary Feeder School
Grade 6 to Grade 9 (Bridge the High School Success)
Grade 4 Grade 5
Gap Analysis
Age 3 to Grade 3 (Every Child Reading by Grade 3)
Conception to Cradle to Age 3
Alumni Associations; Coaching; Networking
Internships; Jobs
College Access; College Credits; Dual Enrollment Apprenticeships; Internships; Mentorships; Industry Certifications
Access to Higher Education
Access to High School; Wrap-Around Services
Access to Early Childhood; Pre-Natal Care; Health Care; Day Care
Research Reflect Respond

PAUSE AND PROCESS

The paths and careers educators pursue are very individual and unique. We have different inspirations for entering the field. Our experiences in classrooms and schools are shaped and influenced by different factors. How we grow and evolve as educators lies at the intersections of our social identities, personal experiences as students, our training and entry points to the field, where we work, our ongoing professional learning, the social-political context of education, and the relationships we develop with students, parents, colleagues, and communities.

Individual Reflection

Take a moment to reflect on your professional journey. When you consider the factors posed, what do you identify as formative aspects of your career?

1. Develop a list of up to ten factors (significant events, policies, people, experiences, opportunities, etc.).
2. Once you have a list you feel demonstrates various formative elements of your development as an educator, identify commonalities between the factors. For example, are there factors that shaped how you think about the purposes of education or factors that influence your relationships and how you develop them?
3. Group the factors you identified together by their commonalities. You may have a factor in more than one group.
4. Look at the groups of factors you have created and consider how they influence your beliefs (about education and learning, students, parents, educators, communities, etc.). What beliefs have developed throughout your specific professional journey?

(Continued)

(Continued)

Collective Planning (in a grade level, department, school, leadership team, parent, community, or other collective meeting space)

Partner with someone in your grade level, content area, school, or at your table. Discuss your list, categories, and how they have influenced and contributed to the development of your beliefs in your professional journey. What commonalities do you find with your partner? Differences? What do you notice about your shared beliefs? What outlying beliefs do you observe?

Continue to aggregate the exploration of your lists, categories, and beliefs until you culminate with a whole-group discussion about what you collectively notice about your shared beliefs.

Additional Resources

Alaska standards for culturally responsive schools: Alaska Native Knowledge Network. Alaska Standards for Culturally Responsive Schools | Alaska Native Knowledge Network. (n.d.). Retrieved January 22, 2023, from https://uaf.edu/ankn/publications/guides/alaska-standards-for-cult/

Wells, L., & Noguera, P. (2012). Comprehensive urban school reform for Newark: A bolder and broader approach. In E. E. Dixon-Roman & G. E. W. Ed (Eds.), *Thinking comprehensively about education: Spaces of educative possibility and their implications for public policy.* Essay. Routledge.

CHAPTER 3

Conscious Collectivism

The Power of the Collective

Being responsible to the community, this is true education.

—Sonia Sanchez

No significant learning can occur without a significant relationship.

—James Comer

In April of 1968, during a speech to the City Club in Cleveland, Ohio, Robert F. Kennedy said the following:

> For there is another kind of violence, slower but just as deadly destructive as the shot or the bomb in the night. This is the violence of institutions; indifference and inaction and slow decay. This is the violence that afflicts the poor, that poisons relations between men because their skin has different colors. This is the slow destruction of a child by hunger and schools without books and homes without heat in the winter.

Although this comment was made in 1968, it bears relevance today in that it describes the persistent impacts of structural racism on Black communities, schools, and students. Kennedy's remarks also reveal the significance of the contradictions, flaws, and limitations that we as individuals carry with us even when working toward a more socially just society. Despite the nation's abysmal record of providing Black students with culturally responsive-sustaining educational opportunities, we educators must remain hopeful and persist in our efforts to do this for our students and ourselves. And we must do so collectively with others.

Education matters not just to the individual children with whose minds we are entrusted but to all of us collectively in schools, neighborhoods, and districts. What is taught and how learning is designed are the blueprint for how society beyond the school functions. Anti-Black content that privileges the historical interpretations, literary and scientific achievements, and social contributions of white people in society while marginalizing or erasing Black people normalizes and reinforces "racist assumptions that (Black) students (are) genetically inferior, never as capable as White peers, even unable to learn" (hooks, 1994). "It socializes White children to see themselves as the ones in power and to develop paternalistic mindsets, strategies, and policies to interact with and control Black people" (Picower, 2021). Learning that emphasizes memorization, test-taking, deficits, classification, and control habituates Black students to limited thinking and creativity, as well as subordinated behaviors. In a study of education policies in Mississippi following the Civil War, education historian Span (2009) observes that the "type of schooling Black children in Mississippi would receive not only determined the status and opportunities for future generations of African Americans but also, indubitably, the future way of life for White Mississippians as well." Schooling does more than build academic knowledge and skills. It shapes how we understand and engage in the life of our society.

Historically, literacy was a collective act and activity for Black people explicitly linked to freedom (hooks, 1994; Muhammad, 2020; Perry, Steele, & Hilliard, 2003). The ability to read and write gave enslaved Black people the power to understand the documents that withheld their freedom and controlled their movements. Bills of sale, manumission papers, emancipation notes, auction notices, and travel passes are documents that frequently appear in popular depictions of Black people acquiring literacy during enslavement. Black people also sought to read and understand the founding documents and state and federal laws that gave legitimacy to the institution of slavery. We pursued literacy at the risk of physical harm, mutilation, or death to change our conditions individually and collectively. Individual freedom requires collective freedom. Both require collective knowledge and collective action.

If we are to reimagine the purposes of public education and envision emancipatory educational ecosystems where Black students—all students—have learning experiences that "create in a person the ability to look at the world for (them)self, to make (their) own decisions," and "act to liberate themselves, and the world, from injustice," we must lean into the collective (Baldwin, 1963; Freire, 2010). Emancipatory educational ecosystems are not simply about changing the conditions—the what—of schooling; it is about creating educational experiences that use lived experiences, cultures, and histories to transform our relationships with ourselves, others, and the world.

The tools of education reform in the "educational survival complex"—school closures, longer school days, high-stakes testing accountability, scripted programs and curricula, and charter schools—have devastating consequences in Black urban communities where contending with historical and contemporary forms of racism is a lived experience. There is a constant struggle between hope and history and vision and reality. Emancipatory educational ecosystems cannot be created, let alone imagined, if we as educators do not build our capacity to engage in this struggle collectively with students, communities, and each other. In this chapter, I offer conscious collectivism as a framework for collaborating and taking action with stakeholders to create emancipatory educational ecosystems and center the strengths, needs, and aspirations of students, educators, and communities.

CONSCIOUS COLLECTIVISM: NOT "ANOTHER" MEETING

Much has been written and researched about parent and community engagement in schools (Eccles & Harold, 1996; Epstein, 2001; Honig, Kahn, & McLaughlin, 2001). The very same deficit beliefs that narrate the educational opportunities of Black students shape most of the approaches, policies, practices, strategies, and expectations applied to engaging their parents and communities (Comer, 1995; Mapp et al., 2022). Among educators, often-heard stereotypes about family and community engagement include "Unfortunately, for many people of color, education is just not a real priority," and "Some parents and families care more about their children's education" (Fergus, 2017). Families and communities are seen and treated as causes of low student performance and impediments to student success. Parent and family engagement efforts tend to myopically focus on helping parents support student learning at home or strengthening connections between parents, communities, and schools. These are important aspects of supporting students academically. They provide information and access to resources parents can use to support learning outside school. But these strategies often target changing the behavior and attitudes of low-income people of color without addressing structural and systemic issues that influence their relationships with schools and us or activating their knowledge to change what we do. The role of families and the community in traditional models of involvement is limited and narrow.

PAUSE AND PROCESS

Individual Reflection

1. What do family and community engagement mean to you?
2. What family and community engagement activities occur in your classroom, school, or district?
3. How are the beliefs you have developed throughout your professional journey evident in your family and community engagement definition and activities? What more do you learn about your beliefs from your family and community engagement definition and activities?

Collective Planning (in a grade level, department, school, leadership team, parent, community, or other collective meeting space)

Partner with someone in your grade level, content area, school, or, at your table. Discuss your family and community engagement definition and activities. What commonalities do you find with your partner? Differences? What do you notice about your shared beliefs?

Continue to aggregate the exploration of your family and community engagement definition, activities, and beliefs until you culminate with a whole-group discussion about what you collectively notice about your shared beliefs.

Over the last decade, increased community-organizing efforts and coalitions addressing the educational conditions Black students—and other students of color—encounter across the nation have shown a spotlight on how traditional models of engagement fail to diminish the inequities and injustices in our educational ecosystems (Mediratta et al., 2009; Stovall, 2016; Warren & Goodman, 2018). Even the most earnest approaches to the engagement of the external stakeholders in our ecosystems struggle to move past traditional family and community involvement strategies to conscious collectivism, which situates external stakeholders as equal partners in the planning, implementation, and evaluation of change. Where the integration of students, families, and communities into transformation efforts has occurred, external pressure from engaged stakeholders and communities has been pivotal (Mediratta et al., 2009). Mary Johnson, chairperson of Parent U-Turn for Leadership in Education, a parent advocacy and training organization in Los Angeles, California, suggests, "Many people write about the need to involve working-class parents in education. Of course, parent involvement is important, but we need to think about how our parents are engaged" (Johnson, 2012).

A community member once shared the following thoughts about their engagement in local education issues with me: "In order to make sense of what is going on, you must be more involved; you have to be involved, attend the meetings, talk to the children, talk to other parents, be involved within the school itself. On the outside looking in, you really won't know what is going on until you participate . . . But when you really become involved within the school, then you understand the mindset of the teachers, the mindset of the kids, the mindset of the teaching system itself, what is going on in general." Based on my work in various roles with stakeholders inside and outside of schools, I understand family and community engagement as a process that builds partnership between all stakeholders to share information (data, strategies, experiences, reflections, etc.), learn together, build a common purpose, set goals and plan, and hold each other accountable for using their collective power, knowledge, and resources to transform schools and the learning that occurs within them. I call this *conscious collectivism*.

Conscious collectivism is more than a meeting or a two-way street; it is a multilane highway with numerous on- and off-ramps that facilitate and support the inclusion and participation of all stakeholders in an educational ecosystem to work together and take collective ownership for the success of Black students and the schools they attend. Families and the community cannot "be involved within the school itself" or active in systemic change if we do not remove the hinges of traditional engagement and let the doors swing open. It requires that schools and districts develop relationships and exchange information with students, parents, community members, and other stakeholders in ways that meaningfully integrate their knowledge, voices, and partnership into school and district initiatives, policies, planning, and decisions. Our interactions with community stakeholders and each other are "shaped by (our) autobiographical stories and by the broader cultural and historical narratives that inform (our) identities, their values, and (our) sense of place in the world . . . and are powerful forces in defining the quality and trajectory" of our work together (Lawrence-Lightfoot, 2004). These autobiographical stories carry the residue we have all accrued from attending schools where deficit beliefs, like white supremacy and anti-Blackness, erase and diminish the significance of Black people in the world. As educators, we are responsible for creating the culture, opportunities, resources, and support that confront the power of these beliefs in our educational ecosystems so that we can work with families and communities as equal partners.

EXAMPLES OF CONSCIOUS COLLECTIVISM

- Open and public policy review and redesign processes where students, parents, and other stakeholders participate in assessing policies for deficit beliefs, contribute to revisions, and provide feedback on final policies.
- A curriculum development process where culturally responsive-sustaining curricula is collaboratively created by teachers in different schools and grade levels in partnership with content experts (Black history, literature, art, local context, etc.) and is then reviewed by students for interest, relevancy, and challenge; it then elicits feedback from parents. Or, further, the curriculum is co-constructed with students.
- At the beginning of the year, co-creating class norms and rituals and routines with students. Small groups work independently, generate ideas, and then conduct presentations to the entire class for input and feedback. The final product is the accumulation of the class's collective perspectives and ideas.

IT'S ALL COLLECTIVE: PLANNING, CONTEXT, AND PURPOSE

In my work with schools, districts, community organizations, and other local partners, I work in three areas to create conscious collectivism: collective planning, collective context, and collective purpose. Collective planning is a participatory approach wherein as many stakeholders as possible work together to build the beliefs and knowledge needed to create emancipatory educational ecosystems. Collective context is the identification and understanding of all the factors that influence and affect the current inequities in an educational ecosystem. Collective purpose comprises the commonly held beliefs, systems, policies, practices, and outcomes that derive from reflecting, assessing, and planning as an ecosystem. All three components of conscious collectivism support and reinforce each other (see Figure 3.1). Collective context is defined through collective planning. The greater the understanding of the collective context of an ecosystem, the stronger the collective purpose becomes (see Table 3.1).

FIGURE 3.1 •

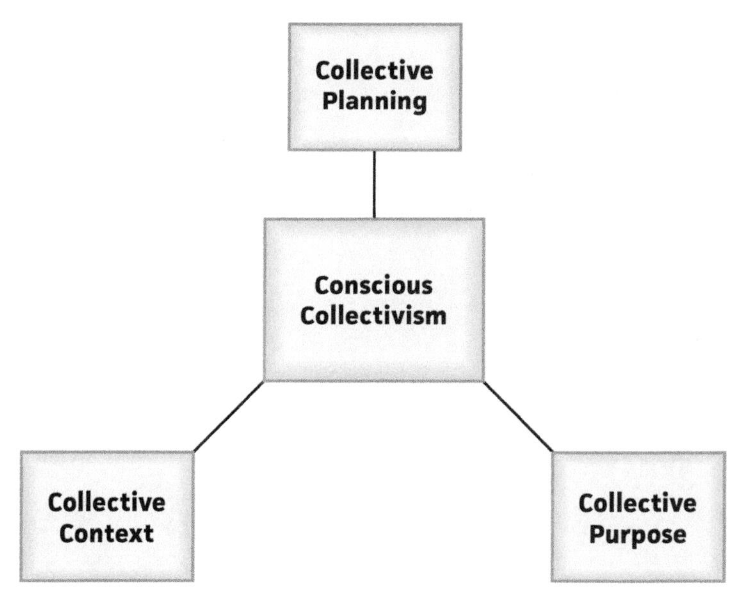

TABLE 3.1 ● Components of Conscious Collectivism

CONSCIOUS COLLECTIVISM		
ORGANIZING COLLECTIVE PLANNING	**DEFINING COLLECTIVE CONTEXT**	**GENERATING COLLECTIVE PURPOSE**
Stakeholders Students Teachers Administrators Parents Community members Partners Businesses Philanthropy Higher education Elected officials **Content Areas** Knowledge building CRSE analysis Root cause & needs assessment Gap analysis Strategy & action planning Alignment **Methods** One-on-ones Focus groups Town halls Professional development Training Participatory action research Advisory groups Planning teams Surveys Testimonials	**Historical/ Social Analysis** Events People Laws Policies Institutions Resources Activities Data Lived experiences Art Archives	**Build** Beliefs Mission Vision Values **Establish** Expectations Norms Roles Goals **Systematize** Collaboration Accountability Alignment Coherence Transparency **Organize** Systems Programs Pedagogy Policies Supports Resources Partnerships

COLLECTIVE PLANNING

Collective planning brings stakeholders together to establish beliefs and knowledge, determine what an educational ecosystem will do to make the shift from educational survival complex to an emancipatory educational ecosystem, and identify how it will reflect on, assess, and measure its progress. Collective planning is where everything takes place. The collective context is understood through collective planning, and the collective purpose is developed through the processes and activities that take place as a part of collective planning. During collective planning, stakeholders

- Engage in participatory research
- Share information (data, strategies, reflections, etc.)
- Learn together
- Challenge old beliefs and build new beliefs
- Give voice to those less heard
- Build a common purpose
- Set goals and plan
- Establish process and outcome indicators
- Hold each other accountable
- Offer testimonials about lived experiences

Collective planning is where the ideas, information, strategies, and relationships that support an emancipatory educational ecosystem are developed. "As groups begin to see themselves and their society from their own perspective and become aware of their potentialities, hopelessness is replaced by hope. Society now reveals itself as something unfinished; it is not a given but a challenge. This new critical optimism leads to a strong sense of social responsibility and of engagement in the task of transforming society" (Freire, 2010). During collective planning, stakeholders practice the interactions and build the trust that is necessary to challenge the prevailing education reforms and replace them with beliefs, policies, methods, systems, and content that create powerful learning for Black students. Table 3.2 provides a description of each of the content areas where stakeholders are engaged in learning, analysis, and planning together.

TABLE 3.2 ● Collective Planning Content Areas

CONTENT AREA	PURPOSE
Knowledge Building	To prime all stakeholders for the learning, process, and work of CRSET
CRSET Analysis	To understand how stakeholders understand CRSET, identify examples of CRSET practice within the ecosystem, and determine what is needed to undertake CRSET
Root Cause Analysis and Needs Assessment	To develop and historically contextualize a holistic understanding of current conditions and inequities
Gap Analysis	To identify what needs to be addressed to move from the current condition to emancipatory educational ecosystems
Strategies and Actions	To plan the strategies and actions that will be taken, identify the resources, and determine how success will be measured
Alignment	To reflect, calibrate, and ensure coherence between the various levels of the system

COLLECTIVE CONTEXT

Defining the collective context of an educational ecosystem develops shared knowledge and localizes the design of an emancipatory educational ecosystem to the histories, strengths, needs, and aspirations of schools, districts, and communities, allowing individuals to make connections across perspectives, experiences, and time periods. Context matters because we use the information in our physical and social surroundings to make sense of our world. Like the context clues we all learned to look for in sentences, the events, people, policies, relationships, location, and resources in our environment give us "hints" that when combined with prior knowledge allow us to understand our settings. Screenwriter Chris Heckmann defines context as "the facts of a situation, fictional or non-fictional, that inspire feelings, thoughts, beliefs, (and behaviors) of groups and individuals. It is the background information that allows people to make informed decisions."

Defining the collective context of an educational ecosystem includes historical/social analysis. Looking closely at historical and social factors helps us understand how our districts, schools, and classrooms are impacted by structural inequality and institutional racism so we can be intentional about planning to disrupt these patterns in our work. Historical/social analysis allows us to attend to the specific ways in which the educational survival complex affects our communities, schools, and students. Critical race theorists in education assert the experiential knowledge of Black people is a necessary, legitimate, and vital element in the dismantling of racial inequality in education and that our stories disrupt the racist discourses on which racial inequality in schools and society is sustained. Historical/social analysis brings these conversations to the foreground through the data, events, laws, and policies that are examined and discussed to generate a shared understanding of the past and its impact on the present. We are then able to use what we learn about how the past affects the existing beliefs, systems, policies, and practices in our ecosystem to guide the future direction of the work. In the words of Newark-based poet and activist Ngoma Hill, "We come for the future. But we won't forget the past" (Hill, 2021).

COLLECTIVE PURPOSE

Very often, we do not understand that it is through the systems and processes we put in place that shared purpose is defined, built, and achieved within our ecosystems. It is one thing to say, "Our purpose is to create emancipatory educational ecosystems where Black student[s] develop the ability to look at the world for (themselves), to make (their) own decisions," and "act to liberate themselves, and the world, from injustice." It is quite another to get your systems, policies, practices, and strategies and the people in your ecosystem thinking and working synergistically toward this purpose.

Collective purpose is what we create through conscious collectivism. It is the collective agreement to work together to eliminate white supremacy and anti-Blackness in our educational ecosystems and to intentionally move toward emancipatory educational ecosystems that affirm Black students. If you have ever led a group of any kind, you know that even when coming together for a common reason—that is, "We want all of our Black students to be successful—there are as many beliefs, definitions, ideas, and strategies among the group as there are individuals. As the work of Carol Lee reminds us, "Cultural communities are communities precisely because of what they share, but at the same time there is always significant variation within communities" (Lee, 2008).

Integrating what everyone brings to a group into a unified understanding of what it means for Black students to be successful, the means to achieve it, and what is necessary to do so is the essence of collective purpose. As I said in Chapter 1, "when people come together to define and understand their shared problems, to excavate and examine their beliefs and values, and to set a course to a new vision of what is possible, they experience the interdependency that exists among all living beings and the environments in which they interact."

Collective purpose is the outcome of the work done through collective planning in a clearly defined collective context. In Table 3.3, I identify the four areas in which I work with schools and districts to help them generate collective purpose. You will notice that developing collective purpose extends beyond building beliefs, mission, vision, and values (the common understanding of "defining purpose"). These are, of course, foundational. But our educational ecosystems are dynamic and fluid and susceptible to internal and external pressures at every level, from the classroom to the school, within and across departments and state departments of education to districts. I include the technical aspects of our work in collective purpose so that they are understood and addressed at the outset with explicit attention to their role in developing and sustaining collective purpose throughout an ecosystem. How many times has a change in policy or an external event negatively affected your work? The technical domains are considered a part of the collective purpose because they organize how we work as educators and, therefore, create the structure of the collective purpose. For example, professional learning communities (PLCs) are collaborative structures that exist widely in districts and schools to analyze and improve classroom practices. PLCs in an emerging emancipatory educational ecosystem would, for example, examine data about staff relationships with Black students and develop measures for validating student work that included students' cultural frames of reference.

TABLE 3.3 ● Generating Collective Purpose

GENERATING COLLECTIVE PURPOSE	
Build	Beliefs Mission Vision Values
Systematize	Collaboration Accountability Alignment Coherence Transparency
Establish	Expectations Norms Roles Goals
Organize	Systems Programs Pedagogy Policies Supports Resources Partnerships

CONSCIOUS COLLECTIVISM IS SYSTEMIC

While the scope of conscious collectivism may appear to be very high level and applicable only at the school and district levels, it is actionable and achievable at the departmental, grade, and classroom levels as well. At the classroom level, teachers engage their students in establishing shared beliefs, setting goals for the class, and designing rituals and routines. Curriculum and learning activities can also be co-constructed with students. Teachers can use individual conferencing to elicit ideas from students or develop teams of students to have leadership over different aspects of the classroom or learning activities. I have also observed community organizations like the Abbott Leadership Institute at Rutgers University-Newark (ALI) employ similar processes as ways to work with stakeholders outside of school to build and plan for collective action in education. Yolanda Greene, manager of Parent Programs for ALI, developed the SUIT UP acronym and framework for her work with parents and other community stakeholders:

- **S**elect the issue and know your rights
- **U**nderstand the system and school challenge
- **I**dentify your allies and build your power
- **T**rust the process
- **U**tilize your strengths
- **P**ersist

The SUIT UP framework used to build community and parent power, which is aligned with the method of conscious collectivism shared in this chapter and our work as educators more than we think, is an example of what conscious collectivism looks like at the community level.

As a part of a vision for emancipatory educational ecosystems, collective planning, collective context, and collective purpose should be applied and supported across our ecosystems. These are practices that can change how we relate to each other, students and families, and communities. Collective planning, collective context, and collective purpose support our ecosystems to work more coherently toward dismantling the marginalizing, individualistic, and oppressive ways in which they have been designed to work for far too long. They support us in sustaining the courage and stamina we need to take the long road. Chapter 4 considers examples of the racialized social dynamics that exist in our society and looks to ecosystems in nature to establish the understanding that ecosystems, including our society, are governed by general principles. Identifying the principles operating in society helps us define the collective context of our educational ecosystems.

PAUSE AND PROCESS

Individual Reflection

1. Describe conscious collectivism in your own words.
2. How is this definition of conscious collectivism similar to or different from how your school or district defines engagement?
3. How does conscious collectivism support or challenge your beliefs?

Collective Planning (in a grade level, department, school, leadership team, parent, community, or other collective meeting space)

Partner with someone in your grade level, content area, school, or at your table. Discuss your responses to the questions about conscious collectivism. What commonalities do you find with your partner? Differences? What do you notice about your shared beliefs?

Continue to aggregate the exploration of conscious collectivism until you culminate with a whole-group discussion about what you collectively notice about your shared beliefs.

Why You Might Resist Conscious Collectivism

1. Deficit beliefs about Black students, families, and communities influence how you perceive their knowledge and role in education.
2. You are seeking a silver bullet for low performance on standardized tests and not to transform the educational ecosystems in which Black students learn.
3. You think addressing issues of race and the socio-historical context of learning is a distraction and takes too long.

(Continued)

(Continued)

Additional Resources

Bergman, E. B., & Mapp, K. L. (2021). *Embracing a new normal: Toward a more liberatory approach to family engagement*. Carnegie Corporation of New York. https://doi.org/10.15868/socialsector.38504

Kuttner, P., Yanagui, A., López, G., Barton, A., & Mayer-Glenn, J. (2022). Moments of connection building equitable relationships between families and educators through participatory design research. *Journal of Family Diversity in Education*, *4*(2). https://doi.org/10.53956/jfde.2022.160

PART II

Collective Context

The chapters in this section bring together concepts from ecological systems theory and models for understanding culture and beliefs to examine the collective context of the "educational survival complex." *Collective context* is the identification and understanding of all the factors that influence and affect the current conditions and inequities in an educational ecosystem. As I discussed in Chapter 3, defining the collective context of an educational ecosystem develops shared knowledge and localizes the work toward emancipatory educational ecosystems to the histories, strengths, needs, and aspirations of schools, districts, and communities.

CHAPTER 4

The Nature of Ecosystems

The crucial thing about an ecosystem is we are all in it. We can't escape it.

—Mindy Fullilove

Indeed, ecological relations are based on meanings; they are semiotic. Ecosystems, no less than cultures, are contingent upon communication.

—Alf Hornberg

We are all in it. Every single one of us is a part of the ecology of our social system, along with everything we create and the plants, animals, raindrops, stars, bacteria, rocks and minerals, and gasses that sustain our lives on this planet. There is no escaping our interconnectedness to each other and the environment for our well-being and survival. We are bound to each other and our environment. This is true at the micro-level, where we interact individually with our families, friends, coworkers, and even the strangers we encounter when shopping at stores, watching sporting events in arenas, seeking help at hospitals, or sitting in our cars when stopped by the police. It is also true at a greater scale where communities interact with each other, ideologies, beliefs, institutions, and resources in the social and physical environment over broad periods of time and, often, great distances. These levels are intertwined with each other and are embodied in both the most mundane activities that make up our daily lives and the unexpected, uncommon, or significant circumstances we experience.

The routine activities of life came to a sudden halt in March 2020, and the coronavirus pandemic became the single-most pronounced example of these intersections in my lifetime.

I returned home from working in a school district on March 12 and, due to health conditions in my family, began quarantining before any local or state mandates required it. On May 25, 2020, George Floyd was murdered by Minneapolis police officer Derek Chauvin, who knelt on Floyd's neck with impunity for over nine minutes while he pinned him to the street next to a police vehicle during an arrest. A video captured by seventeen-year-old Darnella Frazier, who was an eyewitness for the prosecution at the Floyd murder trial, went viral on Facebook the day of the murder. Witnessed by the world through Darnella's eyes and her courageous post to Facebook, this brutal disregard for Black life ignited protests throughout the United States and around the world. In Minneapolis, Nairobi, Paris, Chicago, Hong Kong, Tokyo, Seattle, Karachi, Tehran, Atlanta, Kraków, Helsinki, Memphis, Oslo, Britain, Los Angeles, Madrid, Rio de Janeiro, Phoenix, Mexico, Sydney, Newark, and many other cities, people outraged by Floyd's murder took to the streets in what became a global breath in the name of justice for George Floyd. The protest in Newark ended at the same intersection where the 1967 rebellion occurred after a white police officer beat and arrested a Black taxicab driver named John William Smith. A few days following the Floyd protest, Mayor Ras Baraka and every Essex County police chief took a knee condemning Chauvin's use of force and murder.

I am convinced that the alignment of the coronavirus pandemic and George Floyd's murder is an amplification of the dire reality we face if we do not embrace a deep and intentional understanding of human ecology as the means to disrupt the white supremacy and anti-Blackness that organize the world in which we live. The inequities revealed by the pandemic and mass media exposure of police brutality are unmistakable examples of how these beliefs shape the way we relate to and interact with each other, locally and non-locally, in our society and the world. What happens over here has an effect somewhere over there. Importantly, both phenomena also show the effect and impact of beliefs on the physical, social, and ideological patterns in our society. The surroundings and conditions in which we live, what we call our environment, in turn, reflect these effects. We are used to thinking about the environment as something separate from us—an empty room we occupy and fill with the props and scenes that give our lives meaning. In this view, the environment is the stage where the action of human life is played out. But how we arrange the props, where the players are positioned, and the interactions that occur matter significantly.

The end of Mindy Fullilove's quote at the opening of this chapter captures it quite poignantly for me: "*We can't escape it.*" We are, of course, surrounded by the elements and wonders of nature, plant life, oceans, mountains, minerals and gems, sunlight and rain, for example. But we—like birds, insects, bacteria, and wildlife—are also a part of nature. The environment is the surroundings and conditions in which we live. The evolution of our brains, higher thinking capacity, and sophisticated language skills might lead us to categorize ourselves as separate and distinct from our environment, but really, we are not. It is our higher levels of evolution and cognition that empower us to interact with the environment in ways that other species cannot and to refashion it in ways that reproduce our internal ideas in the physical world. Our environment reflects us. Because of our intelligence and ability to make choices about what we do based on new information, WE, unlike any other species on the planet, have the capacity to determine the nature of our environment. WE, unlike any other species, literally create the world around us. WE get to choose *what* we want our environment to be, *how* we want to interact, *and what* we want our societies to be. The questions for us as educators are as follows: What learning environment do we want to create for Black students? How do we want to be in relationship with Black students, families, communities, and each other? What do we want districts, schools, and classrooms to be for Black students?

DIS-EASE BY DESIGN

Ecology is generally explained as the relationship between nature and organisms, between living (biotic) and nonliving (abiotic) things. As ecological theories continue to evolve, human beings are increasingly understood as among the most important living things in the global ecosystem. Environment is the surroundings and conditions in which we live. Ecology is the organization, patterns, relationships, and interactions that exist between us and all the aspects of our environment. How we as human beings understand our relationship to each other and to our environment has serious implications for the health of our ecosystem as a whole and consequences for us as individuals and groups. The Covid-19 pandemic and the murder of George Floyd chipped the shiny veneer of "equality and opportunity for all" to expose the polarity, division, and inequity that shape relationships and outcomes throughout our ecosystem. Like the GIS maps I discussed in Chapter 1, the impacts of Covid-19 and fatal police shootings look differently depending on zip code. Zip codes with predominantly white high-income communities would show fewer deaths from Covid-19 and much less, if any, fatal police shootings at all. Majority Black low-income communities would demonstrate higher deaths from Covid-19 and greater numbers of fatal police shootings.

Environment is the surroundings and conditions in which we live.

Ecology is the organization, patterns, relationships, and interactions that exist between us and all the aspects of our environment.

Despite rallying cries like "We're all in this together," "We're all in the same boat," or, even, "Everyone can get the virus," the impact of Covid-19 on demographic groups across the country portrays a very different reality. The percentage of Black people who have died from Covid-19 is higher than our percentage of the U.S. population (Elflein, 2023). In Newark, residents living in densely populated neighborhoods, apartments, and multiple-generation households with higher social vulnerability, such as higher levels of poverty and lower levels of education, income, and employment, were disproportionately exposed to social and health risks and, as a result, died at higher rates than individuals in single-family dwellings. Black people experienced higher Covid-19 confirmed case and death rates than counties with higher population percentages of white people. In April 2020, the unemployment rate for Black workers nationally was 16.5 percent compared to 14.2 percent for white workers (Gould & Wilson, 2020). Black workers, disproportionately represented in "employment in grocery, convenience, and drug stores (14.2%); public transit (26.0%); trucking, warehouse, and postal service (18.2%); health care (17.5%); and child-care and social services (19.3%)," were exposed at greater rates to the virus (Gould & Wilson, 2020). The disparate impact of this unanticipated and uncontrollable global health crisis on lower-income Black and Latino/a people in this nation will ripple out for generations, exacerbating already existing inequities in every measure of health and social outcomes.

While longitudinal data on the impact of Covid-19 doesn't yet exist, we can look back over years to identify patterns in racial disparity in fatal police shooting victims. In fact, current data on police shootings demonstrate that even though there is the increased use of body cameras, heightened media reporting, citizen recordings, and social media posts, there has been no reduction in police shootings. From 2015 to 2020, there were 5,367 fatal police shootings. Black people are almost three times more likely and Latina/os are one and a half times more likely to be killed by the police than white people in America. Whether armed or unarmed, Black people are disproportionately killed by the police (Lett et al., 2021). Though it took 9 minutes and 46 seconds of endless time recorded on a cellphone camera to sear this reality into the collective awareness of the nation and the world, Black people have been speaking the names of victims of police shootings year after year and decade after decade. Near the end of my senior year in high school, Phillip Pannell, a high school sophomore, was shot in the back by a police officer in Teaneck, New Jersey, a town adjacent to where I grew up. I knew Phillip. For too many Black people, police shootings are more than live footage streaming to a social media page; they are direct personal experiences that extinguish the lives of people we know and love without sense or meaning. The trauma and mental health issues that result from this unchecked assault on Black life are felt by the families and friends of victims but also by Black people who are not directly connected to the victims or witnesses of the shootings (Lett et al., 2021). Reverberations flow into our communities. So much so, that medical and public health professionals like Dowin Boatright, assistant professor of emergency medicine at Yale, argue "that fatal police shootings of Black people and other people of color are recognized and treated as a public health emergency" (Belli, 2020).

The Covid-19 pandemic and the murder of George Floyd, together with their combined effect on the social climate of the times we are living in now, show us that the organization of our ecosystem is a complex combination of material, societal, and psychological aspects. Through these examples, we can see how different levels of our lived experience and interactions with each other and our environments are inherently biological, psychological, sociological, and geographical. The way the pandemic seeped into nations, communities, and households differently was based as much upon the social and cultural laws by which we live as it was the epidemiology, or natural laws, of the virus's transmission. Black people had the greatest exposure to the virus because of the policies and practices, such as redlining, racial covenants, and predatory loans, that have increased our likelihood of living in poor-quality housing in densely populated cities. I agree with Swedish archaeologist Nilsson (1998), who says, "Our relationship to the environment, and the question of how to deal with the things in it, is dependent upon the information connections between the outer and inner worlds." This then means the social inequities and injustices that exist today and have been reproduced in American society for over four hundred years are the direct result of the way that beliefs, values, and behaviors organize the ecology of our social system and the subsystems—for example, schools—within it. For those concerned with dismantling the white supremacist and anti-Black architecture that erects the laws, policies, and social institutions that shape our society—in our case, public education—the importance of this understanding cannot be overlooked. An ecological lens provides a framework through which we can see the parts of an ecosystem and understand the principles that determine how it is organized and behaves. Let's take a brief look at two examples of naturally occurring ecosystems.

PAUSE AND PROCESS

Individual Reflection

1. How have you experienced the connections, relationships, and systems that exist in our society? Groups? Within groups (i.e., race, gender, socioeconomic status, religion, sexual orientation, etc.)? Across groups?
2. How do your experiences shape your beliefs about yourself and others?
3. Are there any additional beliefs you would add to the existing categories of beliefs you began developing in Chapter 2?

Collective Planning (in a grade level, department, school, leadership team, parent, community, or other collective meeting space)

Partner with someone in your grade level, content area, school, or at your table. Discuss how you experience the connections, relationships, and systems that exist in our society. What commonalities do you find with your partner? Differences? What do you notice about your shared beliefs?

Continue to aggregate the exploration of how you experience the connections, relationships, and systems that exist in our society and beliefs until you culminate with a whole-group discussion about what you collectively notice about your shared beliefs.

ECOSYSTEMS: FROM TINY INSECTS TO GIANT TREES

As I mentioned in the introduction, we can find countless examples of how living things and the environment depend on each other for survival. Looking closely within and across these ecosystems for patterns in organization and behavior illuminates underlying principles that determine how the parts within healthy ecosystems interact with and regulate the stability of the overall ecosystems. Ant colonies and forests and trees are two ecosystems we are all likely familiar with that share a few defining characteristics.

The possible examples of ecosystems I could have drawn from are quite limitless. Explanations of the human body, starlings, aquatic life, and agriculture are at the tip of our fingers on Google. I chose ant colonies and forests and trees because, at some point in my life, I have been intrigued by them but also because, as extremely divergent examples of ecosystems, they share four characteristics I find important to developing an ecology of equity in education.

1. Collective behavior evolves in relation to a dynamic environment.
2. Networks, the amalgamation of individuals into a collective, are key to the adaptation and resiliency of an ecosystem.
3. Difference is natural and everywhere. In evolved ecosystems, diversity enhances the productive exchange of resources and information to ensure the health of the overall system. The more diverse species or components in the ecosystem, the more the system is resilient in the face of threats or changes.
4. Unfettered and ongoing communication among the parts of an ecosystem ensures stable, but nonequilibrium states through feedback and information.

ANT COLONIES

Maybe you have seen trails of ants carrying crumbs on their backs into the mound of their colony. It is captivating to watch. They hustle in and out of those conic holes with unmatched purpose and order, completely undeterred by any obstacle that tries to get in their way. As children, my sister and I used to revel in poking sticks down into the mounds we found in our yard and changing the ants' direction by dousing their paths with water and other liquids. Despite our persistence, our torments of the ants never had any lasting effect. When the liquid dried up, the ants would be back, marching one by one to and from whatever food sources they were foraging (see Figure 4.1). The entrance to their colony would simply reappear.

Ants are often described as ecosystem engineers because they perform many functions vital to our environment. Ants act as decomposers by feeding on organic waste, insects, or other dead animals. They help keep the environment clean. They also carry seeds and help plants disperse into new areas. Entomologists and ecologists argue that we literally cannot live without them.

FIGURE 4.1

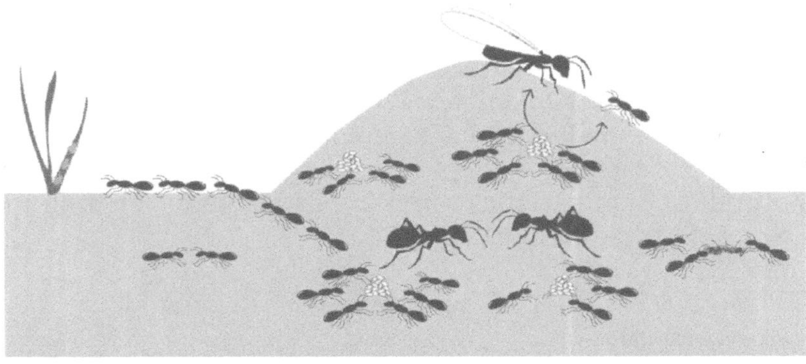

Ants, like some bees, some wasps, and all termites, live in complex societies with defined characteristics. Ant societies have a division of labor, communication between individuals, and the ability to solve complex problems. Ants work collectively to perform many tasks, such as collecting, processing, and distributing resources and finding, building, and defending their nests. Their collective behavior is the result of interactions among individuals (Gordon, 2010).

All ants form trail networks: paths that connect food sources and nests. Depending upon their environment, the formation of trail networks can vary. In unstable environments with high competition for food sources, ants use a system of pheromones (chemical substances that they emit) to amplify their foraging rates, create new trails, and recruit each other. Ants in unstable environments demonstrate the capacity to deal with many kinds of environments, to easily find new sources, and to respond rapidly to threats and disturbances in their environment. Ants in vegetated stable environments, on the other hand, deposit pheromones in ways that keep ants from their host colony together on their trails as opposed to recruiting other ants. In these environments, ants prioritize coherence and increase food collection at local nodes on a path (Gordon, 2014).

Ant development of trail networks in dissimilar environments gives us a line of sight into how different species with common characteristics in their social organization behave in response to their environmental conditions. It shows that, even among one of the oldest insect species on earth, collective behavior evolves in relation to a dynamic environment.

TREES AND FORESTS

Trees are ubiquitous in our lives. A vital resource, they are as important to our existence as food and water. Trees and land plants produce about 30 percent of the oxygen on earth, the rest (70 percent) is produced by plants in the ocean (which are being impacted by polluted water). Trees and other plants keep our air breathable by removing carbon dioxide and pollutants (Krulwich, 2016). They also add moisture through transpiration. We can also recall lessons in school about the many uses for which trees are cut down, including construction, furniture, newspaper, and pencils, as well as clearing for farms and agriculture. Trees are among the oldest and largest living organisms on our planet and, throughout time, have had sacred meaning and purposes to different communities of people. What most of us never learned in school is that trees can talk to one another (see Figure 4.2)!

FIGURE 4.2 ●

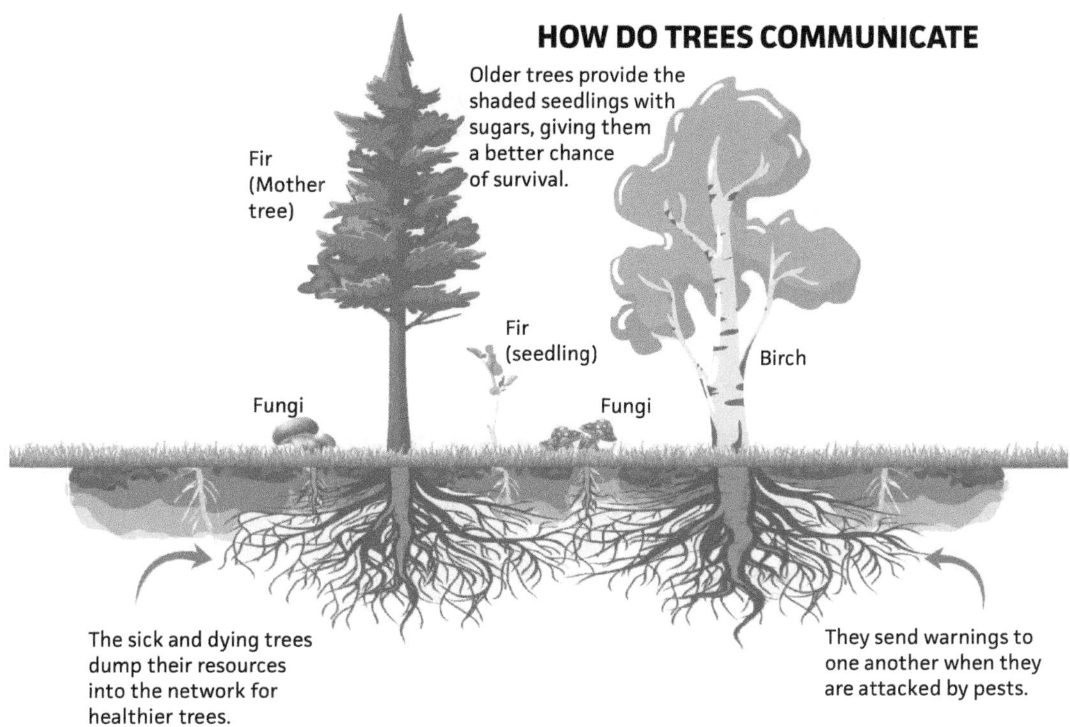

When we think about forests as ecosystems, we tend to do so in terms of the trees, animals, insects, and other organisms that populate them as well as how they contribute to our environment and lifestyles. We think of what we can see and how it impacts us. The work of forest ecologist Suzanne Simard gives us an entirely different perspective on the ecology of forests. Simard reveals a "wood wide web" of communication and cooperation among trees that takes place deep in the earth at the very core of a mycorrhizal (fungal) network (Beiler et al., 2010, 2015). Trees share nutrients and signals through these underground networks. In her groundbreaking research, Simard shows that paper birch and Douglas fir trees use chemicals—such as carbon, nitrogen, and phosphorus—defense signals, and water to share information deep in the soil (Beiler et al., 2010, 2015). At the center of this communication are "mother trees," the oldest and most dominant trees in a forest, which are connected to hundreds of other trees through large root systems that transfer nutrients in these networks. Kinship is recognizable in these networks, as the mother trees pass greater resources to their seedlings. While mother trees provide more support to familial networks they do also share resources with neighbors (S. Simard, 2017). For example, if a species was injured when a neighboring plant is harvested, networked plants upregulate their defense genes and increase defense enzyme production in response to information communicated across the network by the injured tree, making them more resistant to the damage. For Simard, "Forests aren't simply collections of trees, they're complex systems with hubs and networks that overlap and connect trees and allow them to communicate, and they provide avenues for feedbacks and adaptation, and this makes the forest resilient" (Simard, 2016).

CHARACTERISTICS OF ECOSYSTEMS

Collective behavior evolves in relation to a dynamic environment.

Networks, the amalgamation of individuals into a collective, are key to the adaptation and resiliency of an ecosystem.

Difference is natural and everywhere. In evolved ecosystems, diversity enhances the productive exchange of resources and information to ensure the health of the overall system. The more diverse species or components in the ecosystem, the more the system is resilient in the face of threats or changes.

Unfettered and ongoing communication among the parts of an ecosystem ensure stable but non-equilibrium states through feedback and information.

THE POWER OF AN ECOLOGICAL LENS

My goal in this book is to develop a comprehensive understanding of districts, schools, and classrooms as "ecosystems," governed by a multitude of feedback loops that shape the environment in which education occurs as well as the nature of teaching and learning. So there is a link between what happens in our society on large scales, determining the overarching purposes, organization, and practices of schooling, and then—within our communities and districts—where you find actual schools and classrooms, and then—within our schools and classrooms—where student learning takes place. There are many complex and intricate beliefs, systems, roles, relationships, and feedback loops involved. Typically, these scales of the education system are considered connected by laws, regulations, and policies at the federal, state, and district levels. This perspective is quite limited, however, because it casts the ecology of our educational system as purely technical and political and separated from the cultural and normative dynamics that facilitate exchange between the parts of the system (Oakes et al., 1993). When educational change is conceptualized through frameworks that are powered by the beliefs of white supremacy, anti-Blackness, meritocracy, competition, and individualism, transformation is unattainable and the "educational survival complex" is unchallenged. Race Forward, a national organization committed to catalyzing movements for racial justice, reminds us that "racial equity requires willful eradication of policies and practices in our government that deepen the ongoing harm from the legacies of slavery, genocide, segregation and the myriad of racialized and often deadly oppression woven into our institutions across society" (Race Forward, 2020).

White supremacy, anti-Blackness, meritocracy, competition, and individualism are incompatible with the four ecological truths I identify in the ecosystems around us. Therefore, if we hope to change education, we cannot approach it as a technical activity that will be achieved by mandates, carrots and sticks, or programs. We must develop precise analyses of our classrooms, schools, and districts as ecosystems within the educational survival complex and understand how dominant beliefs, culture, and social norms govern our interactions, relationships, and the learning we provide. During this process, we

- Develop an ecological lens
- Identify where and how the beliefs of white supremacy, anti-Blackness, meritocracy, competition, and

individualism operate within classrooms, schools, and districts

- Assess how we individually and collectively facilitate the operation of white supremacy, anti-Blackness, meritocracy, competition, and individualism in classrooms, schools, and districts
- Make individual and collective commitments to dismantle the operation of white supremacy, anti-Blackness, meritocracy, competition, and individualism in classrooms, schools, and districts

In Chapter 5, I consider the intersection of social systems and racial beliefs and ideologies to help make how race operates in our educational ecosystems more visible.

Why You Might Resist Understanding Your Classroom, School, or District as an Ecosystem

1. We've been taught we are separate and that our society cannot thrive without individualism and competition.
2. Boundaries make you feel comfortable and help you create borders between yourself and others.
3. Ideas, policies, programs, strategies, and reforms that emphasize the parts of our work are more prevalent than those that bring the whole into focus.

Additional Resources

Brown, B. (n.d.). *The power of vulnerability.* [Video]. Ted Conferences. https://www.ted.com/talks/brene_brown_the_power_of_vulnerability/transcript?language=en

Lee, C. D. (2010). Soaring above the clouds, delving the ocean's depths. *Educational Researcher, 39*(9), 643–655. https://doi.org/10.3102/001 3189x10392139

CHAPTER 5

There's Race in Our Educational Ecosystems

Because rationalizations have been created to justify the social arrangements, it is easy to believe everything is as it should be.

—Beverly Daniel Tatum

Societal storylines get reproduced and reenacted (and resisted) locally and as they are invoked, academic and racial identities are available, imposed, or closed down (influencing engagement and learning).

—Maxine McKinney de Royston and Na'ilah Suad Nasir

When I started teaching, my feelings swung back and forth on a pendulum between the invincible and the impossible. On the one hand, I wanted my students to reach the pinnacle of their learning. On the other hand, I was confronted daily with the brutal force that the institutional racism of the "educational survival complex" exerted on the school where I worked and the students I taught. I have borne witness to this tension in the work of all the school and district leaders with whom I have worked over the last decade. Racism is institutionalized and operationalized in and through public schools. Yet public education is consistently cast as the leading solution to the poverty, poor health, unemployment, and crime disproportionately impacting Black people. Educators are charged with creating magical classrooms and schools that "beat the odds" and "level the playing field." These expectations are as unrealistic as they are exasperating. It is time we met them with a "hard eyed view of racism" that will give us "the strength and empowerment (we need) in a society that relentlessly attempts to wear us and our students down" (Bell, 1992). To challenge these expectations, there are three areas of growth for educators:

1. Articulate the ways in which our educational ecosystems operate based on race as a social construct.
2. Understand how race is present in the interactions that occur in classrooms, schools, and districts.
3. Challenge and unlearn the beliefs, ideas, and practices that maintain our schools and classrooms as products of the educational survival complex.

While it may be more convenient to view our systems, the policies, and the practices we implement within them as colorblind and meritocratic, doing so continues the cycles of dehumanization and marginalization experienced by Black people. Chapter 5 challenges mainstream ideas about education as neutral and the "great equalizer." It pushes us to understand how our systems are racialized. Just as you would pause before drinking water if someone told you, "There's lead in the water," the title of chapter, "There's Race in Our Educational Ecosystems" is intended to make you pause before assuming your classroom, school, or district does not contain the racial beliefs and ideologies that create racial inequality in our society.

THE ILLUSION OF OPENNESS AND OPPORTUNITY

One Saturday morning nearly ten years ago, I sat in the back of the room during a public advocacy meeting for parents and community members concerned about education in the Newark Public Schools (NPS). These meetings, held monthly by the Abbott Leadership Institute at Rutgers University-Newark for nearly twenty years and well-attended by community advocates, public school parents, students, and college students enrolled in teacher education programs, have been a valuable source of information about public education and reform as well as effective strategies for parent engagement and education advocacy. The topics occasionally draw local teachers or other education professionals—for example, school social workers or guidance counselors attend, as do participants from outside of Newark and the local press. The meetings generally included a presentation about a timely issue facing public education in the Newark Public School district and concluded with ample time for questions from the attendees. On this particular Saturday morning, the question, "Why can't these students just leave their problems at home?" submitted on a sticky note and read aloud by the facilitator during the question and answer section of the meeting evoked side glances and stirred courtside commentary among the attendees. The question has never left me.

I remember thinking at the time, "Who would ask such a question?" This was a group that typically held a more nuanced understanding of the relationship between students' lives and the learning process. I wasn't alone in my surprise. After the facilitator read the question aloud, some of the other regular meeting attendees looked around the room, searching for a guilty face. The nature of the question suggested that it was posed by someone who worked closely with students inside of schools or classrooms. In this audience, this was most likely a college student completing their student teaching in a Newark school. I recall hearing the familiar, "Oh no, they didn't," in response to the complete disconnection and disregard this question expressed about the lived realities of students. I am sure some of you have heard similar questions or comments in professional development sessions, staff meetings, or the faculty room. Some of you may have, at some point in your career, asked or expressed analogous sentiments. In my work with schools and districts, I anticipate that at some point in the process, comments like, "I just want to teach my content," "These students don't want to learn," "These parents don't care about school," or "These communities don't value education" will surface. While remarks such as "Parents should teach their kids to read at home" or "Schools are not social service agencies" may seem harmless to some, they are typically a reflection of deficit thinking and the presumed inferiority of Black people. A more overt manifestation of deficit beliefs about the abilities and capacities of students is simply, "These kids can't learn."

Whether posed as questions or blanket statements, the underlying assumptions in these and other comments like them are rooted in anti-Blackness and deficit views about Black people and supported by mental models that see the students and their families and communities as inherently inferior. Such statements also imply that schools are separate from students' lives beyond the boundaries of their schools, the lives and experiences of school staff, and the sociohistorical and political context in which students exist. They point the finger at people and not at structures or systems, the implications of which suggest a pernicious belief that the Black students sitting in our schools and classrooms are getting the inferior education they deserve and there is not too much that can be done about it. An extension of such beliefs is that if Black people do not value education, then it is acceptable for their children to be taught by uncertified teachers or long-term substitutes, to relegate their learning to memorization and recall, or to employ a one-size-fits-all approach to instruction. Before the desegregation efforts that followed *Brown v. Board of Education*, segregated schools where Black children were taught using outdated and discarded textbooks passed onto them by white schools after they received new curricula materials ensured these assumptions were visible, known, and publicly accepted. Today, while you will not encounter a school marquee that reads, "School for Blacks" or "English Only," in nearly every school you enter, many characteristics of public education bear witness to the contemporary saliency of these assumptions in the curricula, assessments, policies, and interactions Black children and staff experience in schools and classrooms daily.

The idea of schools as "great equalizers" is a conspirator in the validation of these assumptions. It perpetuates the idea that students who are capable and demonstrate "grit" can overcome any of the barriers or obstacles they may confront and will acquire the knowledge and skills they need in school to be successful in life. So why is the idea that education levels the playing field so difficult to unseat? It has long been the case that white women make up the majority of the teaching force and school leadership positions. Over 59,000 Black educators lost their jobs in the decades between *Brown v. Board of Education* and the 1990s (Hudson & Holmes, 1994). At the turn of the twenty-first century, less than 10 percent of teachers were Black. A recent report from the Pew Research Center indicates that "about eight-in-ten U.S. public school teachers (79%) identified as non-Hispanic white during the 2017–18 school year and fewer than one-in-ten teachers were either Black (7%), Hispanic (9%) or Asian American (2%)" (Schaeffer, 2022). Since the early 2000s, the number of teachers over 50 has been on the decline (Ingersoll et al., 2021).

Clearly, most of us working in education today were not born before the Civil Rights Era or the laws and policies it induced. Most of us do not reflect the changing demographics of the nation and our schools. As a result, there is very little firsthand knowledge of the oppressive apparatus that legalized segregation or experiences of institutionalized racism among educational professionals currently working in schools or districts. Despite protests and uproar that suggest otherwise, there is a dearth of thoughtfully developed and historically accurate curriculum and textbooks in K–12 education. Teacher education and educational leadership programs lack culturally responsive and sustaining education and critical race theory courses. Therefore, it is not a stretch to say there are also very few school and district personnel with substantial secondary expertise of the true racial history of this nation and its impact on the education of Black people (Anderson, 1988;

Perry, Steele, & Hilliard, 2003). Moreover, universal access to public schools has obscured the prevalence of overt practices of discrimination (like learning that emphasizes discipline, rote learning, and character education or social emotional learning) and visible barriers. As a result, educators' perspectives about educational opportunity and student achievement are shaped by what Theresa Perry calls "the illusion of openness and opportunity," or the idea that American institutions, like education, are open toward and accept all races (Perry, Steele, & Hilliard, 2003). From this view, Black students' educational attainment is limited by their intellectual inferiority and lack of motivation and not the marginalizing and oppressive educational experiences characteristic of the educational survival complex.

PAUSE AND PROCESS

Individual Reflection

1. What comments or questions have you heard expressed by colleagues, media, or others about Black students during your work in schools?
2. How did you react and/or respond to the comments or questions you identified?
3. What beliefs underlie the comments or questions you identified? What beliefs underlie your reaction/response to the comments or questions you identified?

Collective Planning (in a grade-level, department, school, leadership team, parent, community, or other collective meeting space)

Partner up with someone in your grade level, content area, school, or at your table. Discuss the comments or questions you have heard expressed by colleagues, media, or others about Black students during your work in schools. What commonalities do you find with your partner? Differences? What do you notice about the beliefs you identify? Your reactions to the comment and questions you discuss?

Continue to aggregate the exploration of the comments or questions you have heard expressed by colleagues, media, or others about Black students until you culminate with a whole-group discussion about what all the individuals present notice about their shared beliefs.

UNEQUAL BY DESIGN: ECOLOGICAL SYSTEMS THEORY

As educators, we know that learning is fundamentally about human development. Our work influences the cognitive development of children from early childhood into late adolescence and determines the knowledge, skills, and dispositions they acquire along the path to adulthood. Education sits at the intersection of human development and learning theories as well as the intersection of the people, systems, and institutions with which children interact. In the 1970s, psychologist Urie Bronfenbrenner introduced ecological systems theory (EST), his widely known theory of child development. EST expanded thinking about child development from individual development to a contextual framework that considers the wider factors and influences (the ecology of the theory) that affect how children grow and develop (2005). Bronfenbrenner recognized the limitations of research about child development that did not account for the influence of social context on children. He believed EST would help to improve social policy related to children, adolescents, and their families (Rosa & Tudge, 2013). Bronfenbrenner's ideas emerged alongside the sociocultural and phenomenological theories being developed by Kurt Lewin, Alexander Luria, and Lev Vygotsky. His work, aided by the explanatory power of these learning theories, has had a great influence on early childhood education (Elliot & Davis, 2018). It has also been applied to teacher supervision (Buchanan, 2020) and informed numerous approaches to school reform and education models, including wrap-around supports, community schools, and the Broader Bolder Approach to Education introduced in Chapter 2 (Quinn & Blank, 2020; Wells & Noguera, 2012).

In the previous chapter, I defined ecosystems as all the living things (cells, humans, plants, animals, and organisms) in a given area, interacting with each other and also with their nonliving environments (weather, earth, sun, soil, climate, and atmosphere). Bronfenbrenner's EST identifies the levels at which we interact with our environment and the processes through which we interact with our environment to help us understand how the ecosystem contributes to who we are. According to EST, both the physical aspects of our surroundings as well as social and cultural processes and practices are a part of our environment. This broadens the concept of environment beyond the buildings, landscapes, and natural resources we might quickly call to mind by also encompassing the beliefs, institutions, and systems that organize our lives socially. From this wider view, the interactions occurring between us and our environment can be seen as bidirectional: We influence and are influenced by the settings, institutions, policies, people, and beliefs that intersect with our lives

(Bronfenbrenner, 2005). Or as Carol Lee suggests, "The cognitive, social, physical, and biological dimensions of both individuals and contexts interact in important ways" (Lee, 2008).

The environments we live and grow in also interact with and affect each other. We can all point to the different ways we have experienced our environments interacting with each other, such as the interactions between our home and school environments or between our community and our friends. We may also be able to recall occasions in our lives where settings we did not directly experience have affected us. One such example might be a time when our parents or caretakers' work environment impacted us. Perhaps a change in their employment status triggered a change in our home environment or changes to healthcare policy resulted in increased financial pressure in our home environment.

There are five levels of systems, *subsystems,* included in EST. These systems, in which we live and develop from birth to adulthood are nested from the smallest and most immediate environment (a family or community) to the broadest cultural values, laws, and customs of a society. They are called the microsystem, mesosystem, exosystem, macrosystem, and chronosystem. Table 5.1 defines and provides educational examples for each level.

TABLE 5.1 ● The 5 Levels of Bronfenbrenner's Ecosystem's Theory

SYSTEM LEVEL	DEFINITION	EXAMPLES
Microsystem	A *microsystem* comprises activities and relationships experienced in a face-to-face setting. They also contain other people and often imply systems of belief.	• A child's family, nursery or playgroup, neighbors and their community • The relationship between a child and a principal, teacher, or school counselor
Mesosystem	The *mesosystem* is all about the links and processes that occur between multiple settings. It is a collection (or system) of microsystems.	• Teacher conference with a parent or guardian at the school • A school provides before and after care to accommodate parents' work schedules
Exosystem	The *exosystem* includes the links and processes that exist between two or more settings. Sometimes the setting does not include the developing person but still has an influence on that person and their immediate setting.	• A parent deployed by the military • The relationship between the home and the parents' workplace • The relationship between the school and the neighborhood group

(Continued)

(Continued)

SYSTEM LEVEL	DEFINITION	EXAMPLES
Macrosystem	The *macrosystem* is the social context in which a child lives and grows up and may be thought of as a societal blueprint that includes the beliefs, systems, laws, social structures, and narratives that organize a society.	• The impact of Covid-19 on a child's housing arrangements • School closures due to budget cuts or reform strategies
Chronosystem	The *chronosystem* consists of all of the changes that occur over the lifetime of a person that influence their development, including major life transitions and historical events.	• A child's parents getting divorced • A child being retained in the 9th grade

Adapted from Bronfenbrenner, U. (1992).

EST clarified the complex interrelationships between individuals, systems, and the broader social context and can be applied to observing these patterns in our educational ecosystems. But EST treats race and the racial beliefs that shape our interactions in society narrowly, marring many of the conclusions it has yielded over time by what author Adichie (2009) calls "the danger of a single story." Bronfenbrenner and the cadre of researchers who embraced EST were, like most researchers in the social sciences, colorblind in their study and analysis of the lives of children. They did not examine the role that racial stratification plays in systems and outcomes children experience. While attempting to illuminate the complex interactions that take place within and across systems that influence the lives of children, EST overlooks how the structures and dynamics through which these interactions occur organize a racialized continuum of opportunities and social interactions that differentially support the development of children and youth based on their racial group belonging. Carol Lee argues that to understand what and how people learn the socio-cultural context must be considered within and across all of the interactions that occur among systems and individuals (Lee, 2012). This includes macro-level policies, institutions, and beliefs.

For example, during the late 1990s, Bronfenbrenner et al. (1996) used data for the period between the 1950s and 1960s to publish a series of very influential studies that examined child outcomes in the context of the social movements occurring during this time: the civil rights movement, women's rights movement, and Vietnam War protests. These studies suggested to them that the societal advances spurred by these movements altered the structure and organization of society, thereby provoking chaos in the lives of children and the social institutions with which they most frequently interact—for example, schools. Bronfenbrenner and his contemporaries used race as a control variable to explain differences and variations in outcomes among children. They did not, however, investigate how the diffusion of racial beliefs and ideologies throughout society from the macrosystem to smaller subsystems, like schools and other social institutions or places of work, impacted societal responses to these movements and consequently access to the increased opportunities they were intended to create. While their findings suggested that children were being universally harmed by sweeping social changes, in reality, chaotic conditions, like poverty, lack of access to public institutions, food deserts, and unstable family structures were conditions imposed on Black children enslaved on plantations that persist today through a tapestry of anti-Black legal and social constructs. Beginning with enslavement, a legacy of anti-Black social policies, laws, and practices have saturated the environments in which Black children grow and develop with "frenetic activity, lack of structure, unpredictability in everyday activities, and high levels of ambient stimulation" (Bronfenbrenner et al., 1996). The box that follows provides a few examples of the anti-Black laws, policies, and practices that have shaped the life course of Black children for hundreds of years.

ANTI-BLACK LAWS, POLICIES, AND PRACTICES

- Slavery
- Three-Fifths Compromise
- Slave codes
- Fugitive slave laws
- Sharecropping
- Jim Crow laws
- Lynching
- State voting laws
- Voter suppression
- Redlining
- Racial covenants
- Segregated public schools
- Zero tolerance policies
- School closures
- Bans on books, Black history courses and curricula, and DEI initiatives
- Three-strikes law
- Welfare (Temporary Assistance for Needy Families)
- Child welfare system policies
- Employment and wage discrimination
- Predatory lending

Despite these and other documented examples of anti-Black laws, policies, and practices that have structured Black life in America, the salience of racial beliefs and ideologies in the systems, institutions, and processes with which children interact is largely ignored. In Chapter 4, I defined the environment as the surroundings and conditions in which we live and ecology as the organization, patterns, relationships, and interactions that exist between us and all the aspects of our environment. Laws, institutions, policies, and relationships mold our environment and shape our interactions. The reoccurring and prolonged forms of interaction that occur in children's immediate environments are the engines of child development in society and in our educational ecosystems. For instance, parent–child activities, teacher–child interactions, and participation in educational activities are examples of recurring, prolonged interactions. Feeding or comforting a baby, playing with a young child, children playing together or alone, caring for others, making plans, and acquiring new knowledge and skills are other familiar types of interactions that take place in children's most immediate environments.

Because children live their lives enmeshed in the interactions between and among systems, their worlds are influenced by each system independently and by the various ways in which these systems interact. Classrooms, schools, and districts are individual ecosystems nested in larger ecosystems. Figure 5.1 depicts the educational ecosystem from the classroom level (micro) to the federal level (macro) and describes the interactions that occur within and across the different levels. The systems represented in this graphic are nested from the smallest and most immediate environment in which students learn (classroom) to the broadest system that impacts student learning at the classroom level (federal).

FIGURE 5.1

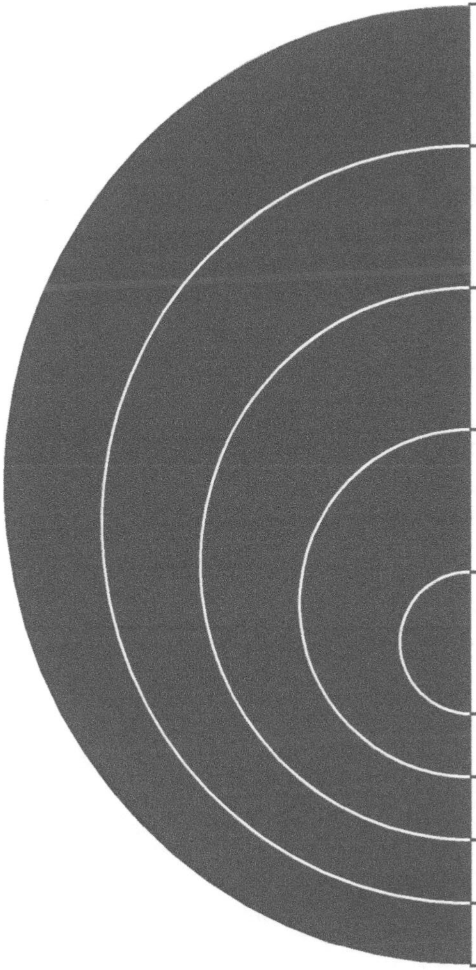

Neighborhood	The neighborhood context of the classroom and schools, where students learn, for example, historical context, local organizations, businesses, and local beliefs about and approaches to education.
School	The interactions that occur between the classroom setting and the school environment, for example, school policies, professional development, or resources for extracurricular opportunities.
Department	The interactions that occur between the classroom setting, grade levels, and the school, for example, curricula mapping, common planning, and professional development.
Grade Level	The interactions that occur between the classroom setting and teachers and students in the same grade levels, for example, recess, assemblies, lessons, common planning, and after-school activities.
Classroom	The interactions that occur with the classroom setting.

Schools and classrooms are educational ecosystems where developmental processes occur. Every aspect of education contains at its core specific face-to-face relations and mediated activities that fuel students' cognitive development through the design, organization, and delivery of learning. Table 5.1 identifies relationships between a child and a principal, teacher, or school counselor as key developmental processes in schools. However, within schools and classrooms, the interactions that influence development also include peer-to-peer relationships, individual engagement with content and learning strategies, group learning, student schedules, teacher assignments, and extended-learning activities. Instructional time, social emotional feedback, and classroom management learning are examples that involve teacher–student interactions. All these interactions are shaped by the individual beliefs we hold as educators as well as in the beliefs present in the systems, policies, and practices in place in our ecosystems. The belief that Black children are not as smart as white children leads to less meaningful dialogue and engagement in their learning, the elimination of arts and elective courses, increased time on basic skills, and zero-tolerance policies. The belief that Black students have innate intellect and talent as evidenced by their creativity and resilience creates opportunity for their voices and expression in their learning, situates learning in their lives, empowers their strengths in demonstrations of learning, centers the significance of their history and culture throughout their learning, and struggles to eliminate toxic policies and practices (Jackson, 2010). Figure 5.2 depicts Central High School from an ecological perspective. Central High School, discussed in more detail in Chapter 2, was the anchor school in a collective effort to improve seven schools in Newark called the Newark Global Village School Zone (NGVSZ). The students at Central were immersed in symbols, experiences, content, and relationships that communicated in this school they mattered. This figure illustrates Central High School's implementation of beliefs that value Black students in the context of a larger educational ecosystem, the educational survival complex, which does not.

FIGURE 5.2

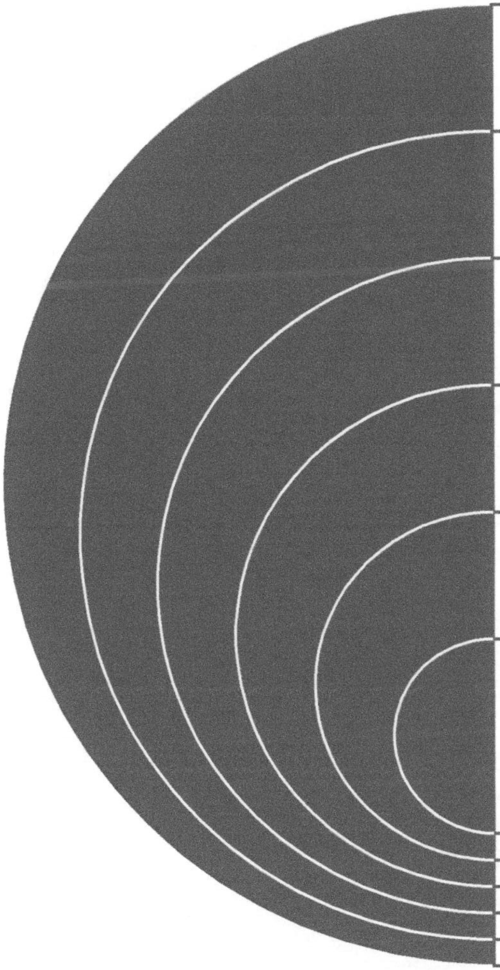

United States	President Barack Obama, Secretary of Education Arne Duncan, Race to the Top, No Child Left Behind Act, School Improvement Grants, Title I, Office of Civil Rights
New Jersey	Governors Jon Corzine and Chris Christie, 76% White, 16% Latino/a, 15% Black, 8% Asian, *Abbott v. Burke*, NJDOE control of Newark, Paterson, and Jersey City, New Jersey Core Curriculum Content Standards, High School Proficiency Assessment, Charter School Expansion, Unenforced Amistad Legislation
Newark	Mayor Cory Booker, 54% Black, 30% Latino/a, 30% immigrant population, 5 wards, downtown development, average income $27,038, largest city in New Jersey, third oldest city in the nation, charter school expansion
Newark Public Schools	14 years of state control, Dr. Cliff Janey is state-appointed superintendent, Great Expectations 3-Year Strategic Plan, Newark Teachers Union, 59% Black, 34% Latino, 7.8% ELL, 8.5% IDEA, 85% FRPL, Partnerships included Cambridge Assessment, AED, Bank Street College, and Scholastic
Central Ward of Newark	Newark Global Village School Zone, six preK to grade 8 schools, one high school, 3,500 school-age children, over 90% Black students, median household income $11,000, 1967 rebellion, part of NPS school leadership team
Central High School	Principal Ras Baraka, 92% Black, 8% Latino/a, 5.8% ELL, 15% IDEA, 80% FRPL, founded in 1911, relocated to new school facility in 2008, culturally responsive-sustaining practices, cultural symbols and historic figures prominent in the school culture and environment, centered relationships, integrated culturally relevant content into the mandated curriculum, community organizations and leader embedded in school community, SIG, SIG monitor

PAUSE AND PROCESS

Individual Reflection

1. How would you describe the connections, relationships, and interactions that occur in your educational ecosystem?
2. How does applying EST impact your understanding of the connections, relationships, and interactions that occur in your educational ecosystem?
3. What factors (social-historical, policies, laws, practice, etc.) can you identify that impact the connections, relationships, and interactions that occur in your educational ecosystem? What is their impact?

Collective Planning (in a grade-level, department, school, leadership team, parent, community, or other collective meeting space)

Partner up with someone in your grade level, content area, school, or at your table. Discuss the connections, relationships, and interactions that occur in your educational ecosystem. What commonalities do you find with your partner? Differences? What do you notice about the impacts you identify?

Continue to aggregate the exploration of the connections, relationships, and interactions that occur in your educational ecosystem until you culminate with a whole-group discussion about what you collectively notice about the impact of these factors.

RACE SHOULD BE VISIBLE IN OUR WORK

Education researchers have dedicated innumerable hours to documenting the inequitable distribution of resources and opportunities that exist in public education. Prudence Carter, a well-known education researcher, argues that "collectively these various spheres of context constitute an *ecology of inequity*, which captures the independent system of economic, social, and political processes at the macro, meso, and micro levels of our society" (Carter, 2018). As legal scholar Derrick Bell states in his groundbreaking call for *racial realism*, "In spite of dramatic civil rights movements and periodic victories in the legislatures, Black Americans by no means are equal to whites" (Bell, 1992). Bell, like many scholars across fields, points out that the decreased visibility of the more obvious markers of racial inequality, such as legally sanctioned segregated seating on buses or Jim Crow signs demarcating access to public spaces, encourage the idea that racism and the racial inequalities it produces are "a thing of the past." Narratives about the diminishing role of race are particularly observable in the discourse about public education that position Black children's access to education in a free publicly funded school as symbols of the elimination of racial barriers to educational opportunity and greater life outcomes. As a result, the disparities in the education attainment of Black youth are perceived as the consequences of self-defeating cultural values and behaviors—such as crime, lack of trust, lack of family values and role models—rather than persistent structural barriers. Deficit views like this affect the interactions that take place in school. For example, they appear in how we speak to students, where we seat students in classrooms, who we call on and when, how we discipline, and the types of curricula, programs, and enrichment opportunities we choose for students.

In her article "From Racial Liberalism to Racial Literacy in Education," Guinier (2004) states that this kind of thinking "positions the peculiarly American race "problem" as a psychological and interpersonal challenge rather than a structural problem rooted in our economic and political system." Our reliance on social science research and data that is colorblind is another barrier to understanding and removing the systemic and institutional racism that sustains inequities in our educational ecosystems. Moreover, such colorblind methodologies often lead to policies and practices that substitute one form of discriminatory conduct (for example, segregated schools) for subtler, though no less discriminatory form (such as tracking and the disproportionate placement of Black students in special education) (Bell, 1992).

In *Street Data: A Next Generation Model for Equity, Pedagogy, and Transformation,* Safir and Dugan (2021) ask, "What if, because of what we deem valid and reliable, we have been asking the wrong set of questions?" It is precisely because of racism's persistent ability to adapt and shapeshift to fit new social, political, and economic contexts that we educators must become equipped to explicitly name and ask questions about racial beliefs, ideologies, and constructs as features of the educational ecosystems in which we work and our individual practices. We must also be prepared to design and implement educational policies, programs, and strategies within our educational ecosystems that will make race visible and "will be more likely to remind those in power that there are imaginative, unabashed risk-takers who refuse to be trammeled upon" (Coates, 2015). In Chapter 6, I examine the influence of culture on our educational ecosystems and draw from my teaching and high school experiences to provide examples of Love's conceptualization of the educational survival complex.

Why You Might Resist Acknowledging There's Race in Our Educational Ecosystems

1. Examining how race works in our educational ecosystems challenges the widely held societal norm that we should be color-blind.
2. It is easier to choose to focus on individual bias than it is to examine systemic racism.
3. When you acknowledge how race works in our educational ecosystems, you can either take personal responsibility for addressing it or be complicit by not addressing it.

Additional Resources

Safir, S., & Dugan, J. (2021). *Street data: A next-generation model for equity, pedagogy, and school transformation.* Corwin Press.

Sue, D. W. (2016). *Race talk and the conspiracy of silence: Understanding and facilitating difficult dialogues on race.* John Wiley & Sons.

CHAPTER 6

Culture, Beliefs, and Emotions in Our Educational Ecosystems

All this is to say that all life is interrelated. We are caught in an inescapable network of mutuality; tied in a single garment of destiny. Whatever affects one directly, affects all indirectly.

—Dr. Martin Luther King Jr.

Human functioning cannot be understood in its wholeness without understanding how biology and human culture work in tandem.

—Carol D. Lee

Learning should be exciting and joyful. Learning is what our brains fundamentally wire us to do. As we interact with people and the environment around us, have new experiences, encounter challenges and overcome obstacles, and engage with new information and ideas, the neurons in our brains receive and exchange information, strengthening some connections and pruning others (Sousa, 2017). As the saying goes, "Neurons that fire together, wire together." When we internalize new information or have a new experience, our nervous systems are activated by a series of biochemical processes that flush our bodies with neurotransmitters. Emotions regulate learning and memory. The stronger the emotion, the greater the memory. If the information or experience is positive or affirming, positive emotions are generated, our cognitive functioning is increased, and our bodies release brain chemicals such as oxytocin, serotine, dopamine, and endorphins. If the information or experience invokes feelings of inadequacy, fear, or failure, negative emotions affect brain function, and learning is hijacked by adrenaline, cortisol, and norepinephrine (Jensen, 2005). Whether we are aware of it or not or, for that matter, want to believe it, emotions matter to learning. The culture we create in our educational ecosystems contributes to the emotions that exist in our classrooms, schools, and districts.

In this chapter, I provide examples of how anti-Black culture operates in Love's "educational survival complex" and the types of experiences and feelings it creates for Black students, including in my own high school. The chapter discusses deficit beliefs and their role in creating anti-Black toxic cultures in our educational ecosystems. I draw from focus groups with students and teachers from an East Coast urban district to provide insights about both the feelings they experienced in their schools and classrooms as well as those feelings they would like to have. This chapter will help you make connections between how culture, beliefs, and emotions impact our educational ecosystems and learning.

THE CULTURE OF LEARNING IN THE EDUCATIONAL SURVIVAL COMPLEX

In *We Want to Do More Than Survive: Abolitionist Teaching and the Pursuit of Educational Freedom* (2019), former teacher and scholar Bettina Love states, "Education is an industry that is driven and financially backed by the realities that dark children and their families just survive." Love goes on to describe the educational survival complex as the dominant educational model, which functions on scarcity and competition, is dehumanizing and punitive, educates Black children as if they, their communities, and their histories do not matter, and is saturated with "racist, anti-dark, emotionally, and physically violent school incidents" (Love, 2019). These are the educational conditions that hijack the joy of learning from many of the 7.4 million Black students enrolled in public elementary and secondary schools today.[1]

The educational survival complex is a toxic educational ecosystem that forces students, families, communities, and educators to exist in a culture of "survival." In this state, the sympathetic nervous system operates in overdrive, making it impossible for the magic of teaching and learning to seamlessly occur (Jensen, 2005). The consequences of this reality are particularly

[1]The student demographics of public schools comprise 13.8 million Hispanic, 7.4 million Black, 2.7 million Asian, 2.2 million of two or more races, 0.5 million American Indian/Alaska Native, and 180,000 Pacific Islander.

detrimental when mainstream narratives about public education proliferate ideas about education as "the great equalizer," yet Black students and their families and educators have experiences that counter this folk mythology. The "great equalizer" narrative about education is gaslighting. It manipulates educators, students, families, and communities into questioning the legitimacy of the perceptions and experiences we have of the anti-Blackness in our educational ecosystems.

In Chapter 1, I described High Point High School, where I became an educator. This school is a prime example of the type of school culture Love indicates the educational survival complex is designed to create for Black students living in a predominantly low-income, urban neighborhood. High Point also demonstrates the working conditions the educational survival complex requires educators to navigate and endure.

High Point is an example of how schools function as a microcosm of the culture of our society. The school mimicked the anti-Black beliefs, ideologies, and experiences that dehumanize other Black people in society while socializing students and their families and educators to accept these conditions. High Point's practice of asking students for their student ID numbers and not their names when they were moving too slowly or cutting class in the hallways is a particularly powerful example of the school's dehumanizing and othering culture. The long lines of students waiting in rain or snow to enter the school in the morning and the bags of garbage I observed in the cafeteria during lunch expose policies and practices that acclimate Black students to their dehumanization. During a diagnostic review of another predominantly Black school in a Southwestern city, several colleagues and I were stunned and appalled to see bathroom stalls in the girl's bathroom without doors and toilet paper. In this school, not only were girls required to ask their teacher for toilet paper before going to the bathroom, but once there, they had no privacy.

But these conditions are not limited to schools in hypersegregated urban communities. The educational survival complex Love describes parses out opportunities such that Black students have entirely different learning experiences than their white or Latino/a peers when in the same school. Black students encounter divergent opportunities within predominantly Black schools in suburban communities. I attended a public high school in Bergen County, New Jersey, the wealthiest and most densely populated county in New Jersey. The predominantly white city where I grew up, home to the most Black residents in the county, was residentially segregated by both race and income. There were four elementary schools, one located in each ward of the city, and one middle and high school. Students primarily attended neighborhood elementary schools, which reflected the residential composition of the ward where we lived. My elementary and middle schools were led by Black principals, all of whom had doctorates. Many of my teachers were Black. From the fifth grade, when my family moved to New Jersey, through high school, most of my classmates were also Black. The high school at one point enrolled a mix of Black and white students from varying socioeconomic backgrounds. But by the time I entered the ninth grade in 1985, the racial composition of the high school was 11.8 percent white, 66.2 percent Black, 17.8 percent Hispanic, and 3.9 percent Asian (Civil Rights Data Collection, n.d.).

My classmates and I attended a predominantly Black high school in one of the wealthiest regions of the country and experienced how the educational survival complex molds itself to the local context of schools, districts, and communities. In 1985 (the year I began high school), white families from a town I will call AC, an adjacent predominantly white town with a sending relationship to my high school, pursued litigation to legally terminate the existing sender–receiver agreement, which allowed them to send their children to the high school tuition free. Instead, they sought to send their children to another adjacent predominantly white and higher-income school district. In 2005, the New Jersey Supreme Court ruled against the AC families and required my school district to find an alternative solution to the racial imbalance in its predominantly Black high school.

My entire high school experience occurred in the pressure cooker of this case, as did the learning of the other students who attended the school over the twenty years it was litigated. My classmates and I were immersed in the narrative that our school could only work if it included white students and white families and no measure was too great to get them back (Jones-McGowan, 2011). Instead of creating a culture that valued, celebrated, and empowered us, the district and school embarked on a mission to prove it could control us and, in so doing, convince white families to be comfortable with their children attending school with us. The district brought in a white male principal from New York to replace the school's Black female principal, a former teacher in the district, who knew the community and school's history. Greater restrictions were placed on us, including zero-tolerance policies, which resulted in more detentions and suspensions. Teachers with connections to the community, school, and students and who had greater teaching experience left the school. The significance of the district's tracking system was amplified as the school focused more on increasing standardized test scores to verify our intellectual ability. Within this culture, division and labeling among the students became pronounced. Another former and popular student, who graduated the year before me, said to me twenty years later, "We all knew who was going to make it. All of you kids who lived behind the high school were the ones that were supposed to make it."

I have four cogent memories of the culture of my high school. First, which speaks to my schoolmate's observation, the students in honors and AP were mostly students, like me, who came from solidly middle- or upper-class Black families. During lunch, gym, and elective courses, students in special education classes, mostly Black boys, emerged from the basement where all the special education classrooms were located. The school did not offer one single Black history or literature course. Finally, as the case progressed, my high school became the target of terroristic threats and on numerous occasions the entire school would be evacuated so that the police could conduct bomb searches. The high school experience my classmates and I had was loaded with microaggressions and outright aggression that made us feel stigmatized, marginalized, unsafe, unvalued, and anxious.

PAUSE AND PROCESS

Individual Reflection

Take a moment to reflect on your educational experience as a student. What aspects of your experience impacted you most as a student?

1. Develop a list of up to ten factors (social identity, significant events, policies, people, experiences, opportunities, etc.)
2. Once you have a list that demonstrates various impactful elements of your educational experience, identify commonalities and group your responses.
3. Categorize your responses together by their commonalities. You may have a factor in more than one group.
4. Look at the categories you have created and consider how they influence your beliefs and behaviors as an educator (about education and learning, students, parents, educators, communities, etc.).

Collective Planning (in a grade level, department, school, leadership team, parent, community, or other collective meeting space)

Partner up with someone in your grade level, content area, school, or at your table. Discuss your list, categories, and how they influence your beliefs and behaviors as an educator. What commonalities do you

(Continued)

(Continued)

find with your partner? Differences? What do you notice about your shared beliefs and behaviors? What outlying beliefs and behaviors do you observe?

Continue to aggregate the exploration of your lists, categories, and beliefs until you culminate with a whole-group discussion about what all the individuals present notice about their shared beliefs and behaviors.

THE DEPTH OF CULTURE WITHIN US AND OUR SCHOOLS TOO

A First Nations proverb says, "No tree has branches foolish enough to fight amongst themselves." Branches on a tree do not compete or separate themselves from each other because they are derived from the same source, the same roots. We have been taught to believe that white supremacy, anti-Blackness, individualism, competition, and meritocracy are natural and even ordained (Weber, 2002). Yes, each of us is part of kinship groups that begin with our immediate families and radiate out over generations to include those to whom we are related by blood and marriage. We call our ancestors our "roots." Phenotypically our kinship groups and societies have evolved differently based on geography and climate. Despite our preoccupation with observable surface differences such as skin color, hair texture, and facial features, it is well-established that we can all trace our roots back to a single species over three million years old, most known as "Lucy," whom anthropologists discovered in Ethiopia in 1974 (Johanson, 2004).

Race is a construct that was created during the seventeenth century to establish white dominance over Indigenous and African people and to codify hierarchy and division in the social relationships, access to resources, and rights that have been carried forward since (Montagu, 2008). The construction of race normalized "white" as the standard bearer of humanity and defined other groups as deviant, deficient, and aberrant to this "norm." It created a culture of white supremacy that is sustained today through language, images, resource distribution, notions of meritocracy, and institutions, policies, laws, and social practices. Racism is a belief system that is built on this false classification of people for the purposes of establishing and maintaining power and privilege over others (Kendi, 2017).

In the introduction, I provide this definition of white supremacy: "White supremacy is 'the all-encompassing centrality and assumed superiority of people defined and perceived as white, and the practices based upon that assumption." It "assigns values to real or imagined differences in order to justify the perceived inherent superiority of whites over People of Color that defines the right and power of whites to dominance" and operates as a "global system that confers unearned power and privilege on those who become identified as white while conferring disprivilege and disempowerment on those who become identified as people of color" (DiAngelo, 2017; Allen, 2001; Solorzano, Perez, & Huber, 2020).

We are exposed to white supremacy and the anti-Black culture and racism it creates when we take our first breath and absorb it throughout our lives from television, textbooks, magazines, childhood songs, food, social media, and as High Point demonstrates, institutions (Okun, 1999). Though white supremacy is the dominant cultural frame in our society, it does not have to be our destiny. When we understand what culture is and how it works in our educational ecosystems, we can create countercultures where Black students are meant to thrive.

FIGURE 6.1 • Zaretta Hammond's Culture Tree

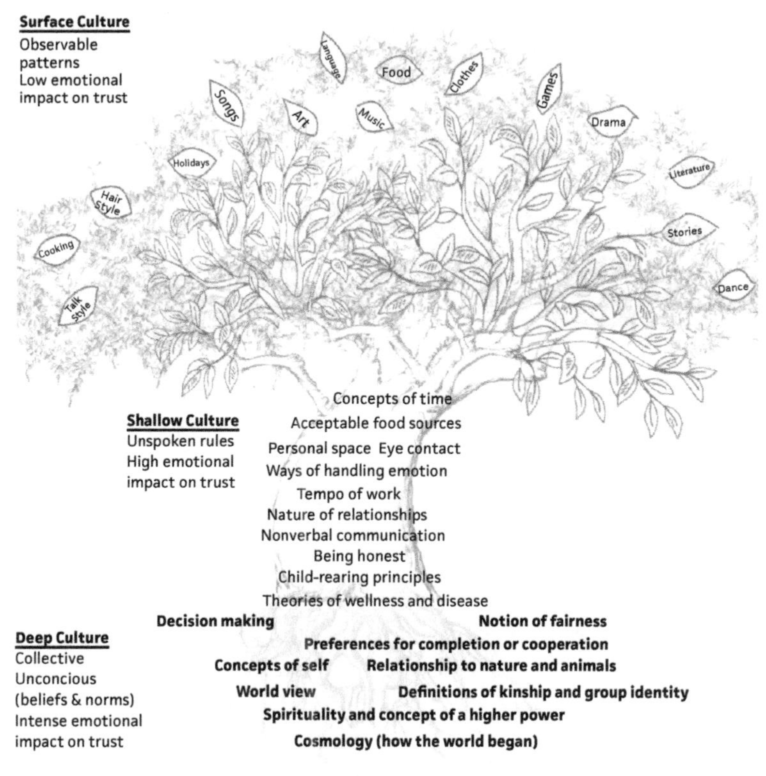

Adaped from Hammond, Z. (2015).

The culture tree in Zaretta Hammond's book *Culturally Responsive Teaching and The Brain* depicts three levels of culture using the metaphor of the tree (see Figure 6.1; Hammond, 2015). *Surface culture*, the observable behaviors that people share, such as holidays, food, music, language and talking styles, and dress, is depicted as the leaves on the tree branches. The trunk of the tree represents *shallow culture* (as distinguished from surface culture, represented by the leaves and branches), which is the unspoken rules around everyday social interactions and norms—for example, social distance, eye contact, conceptions of time, or views about work. The roots of Hammond's culture tree represent *deep culture*. Deep culture is the beliefs, norms, and values that are shared among groups of people. In Hammond's representation of culture, the aspects of deep culture work together in what she identifies as the collective unconscious. Conceptions of self and others, definitions of kinship and group identity, and preferences for competition or collaboration are aspects of deep culture. Deep culture is transmitted through the roots of Hammond's tree, like the roots of trees in a forest communicate and share information for defense and survival.

Hammond offers this very useful explanation of culture: "culture is like software that programs our 'hardware' (the brain). Cultural values and learning practices transmitted from our society, communities, and families guide how the brain wires itself to process information and handle relationships. Neural pathways are over-developed around one's cultural ways of learning." At the organizational level, this metaphor can be applied to the deep culture and collective unconscious of an educational ecosystem. The cultural practices that organize learning in classrooms, schools, and districts establish the expectations that guide how we collectively process information in our educational ecosystems as well as how we perceive and develop relationships with each other. In the same way that repetition and practice build and strengthen our individual neural pathways, the beliefs, rituals, routines, messages, relationships, policies, and practices that create the culture of our educational ecosystems engage all stakeholders in a collective culture that repeatedly exposes us to its values, expectations, and behaviors. Curriculum choices exhibit culture. Practices for engaging and partnering with parents and community are driven by culture. The core learning methodologies and strategies are culture. The culture of an educational ecosystem is the basis for which resources are distributed, students are disciplined, and staff feel about themselves and others. The culture of your educational ecosystem thus becomes the software that programs it. The culture of our existing education paradigm is programmed with white supremacy, anti-Blackness, individualism, meritocracy, and competition. Zaretta Hammond's culture tree helps us visually see that to change the software running in our educational ecosystems, we must dig up the roots and change the beliefs that exist within them. In other words, to change what we can see and observe (the leaves), we must change what we cannot see and directly observe (the roots).

THE SIGNIFICANCE OF DEFICIT-THINKING IN OUR EDUCATIONAL ECOSYSTEMS

White supremacy culture promotes widespread deficit-thinking about Black people in schooling, entertainment, media, and day-to-day interactions. Education scholars Lori Patton Davis and Sam Museus define deficit thinking as "a blame-the-victim orientation that suggests that people are responsible for their predicament and fails to acknowledge that they live within coercive systems that cause harm with no accountability" (Davis & Museus, 2019). As a result, the solutions to social problems that stem from deficit thinking are directed at fixing groups of people and not the systems and structures that determine opportunity and resources. Deficit thinking, also interchangeably referred to as deficit beliefs, deficit framing, deficit paradigms, or deficit perspective, is endemic to how American culture views and treats Black people in the United States and globally. "Black families aren't motivated to do better" and "There are no Black kids in our school that are gifted and talented" are examples of how deficit beliefs and ideology impact social policy. Here are a few other examples of prevalent deficit ideologies that have a major influence on social policies:

- Individuals' traits are the source of their own failures.
- They don't care about their community.
- Low-income families do not value education.
- People on welfare don't want to work.
- Parent and community engagement don't matter here.
- Immigrants are a major source of crime.
- We have to be the students' parents, social workers, and teachers.
- The police are necessary in order to protect us from them.
- If students don't assimilate, they can't be successful.

The deficit beliefs in an educational ecosystem figure that follows uses the first deficit belief from the preceding examples and demonstrates how beliefs flow through the levels of an ecosystem (see Figure 6.2).

FIGURE 6.2 •

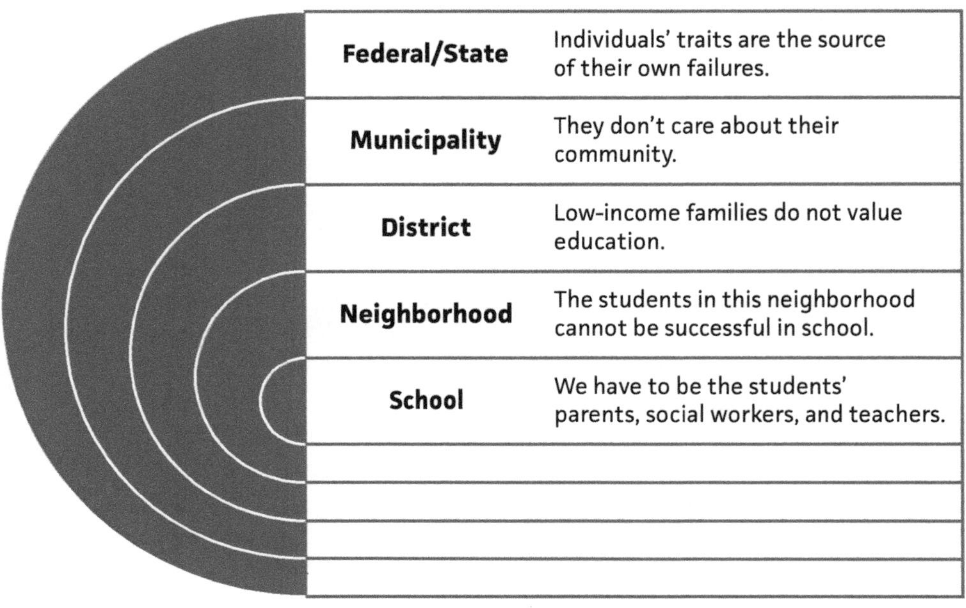

Deficit thinking pathologizes Black communities, schools, and students and casts us as cultural, social, economic, and political problems in an otherwise successful system. Research about educators' beliefs of Black students shows that Black students are subjected to harsher discipline, called-on less frequently, provided assignments with less cognitive demand, recommended less for gifted and talented, and given less praise and patience as a result of deficit beliefs (Elhoweris et al., 2005; Morris, 2016; Tenenbuam & Ruck, 2007; Villegas, 2007). Beliefs, ideas, and language are at the core of how we conceptualize each other and the world we live in. Whether in classrooms, leading schools and districts, writing curriculum, running nonprofits, or developing policy, deficit beliefs dominate the work of educators. Deficit beliefs and the language, policies, and practices that reinforce them shift attention away from drawing out the brilliance of Black students to identifying, labeling, and fixing weaknesses. The highly acclaimed school leader, author, and equity advocate Kafele (2019) argues that "DEFICIT speech in schools that reflect DEFICIT thinking produce a DEFICIT culture that puts children at a DEFICIT."

PAUSE AND PROCESS

Individual Reflection

1. What have you been taught to believe about Black people? Other people of color?
2. Where did you learn these beliefs?
3. Are most of the beliefs you identified deficit based or positive beliefs? Why do you think this is?

Collective Planning (in a grade level, department, school, leadership team, parent, community, or other collective meeting space)

Partner with someone in your grade level, content area, school, or at your table. Discuss what you have been taught to believe about Black people and other people of color. What commonalities do you find with your partner? Differences? What do you notice about your shared beliefs? What outlying beliefs do you observe?

Continue to aggregate the exploration of what you have been taught to believe about Black people and other people of color until you culminate with a whole-group discussion about what you collectively notice about your shared beliefs.

BELONGING, PURPOSE, AND PRIDE

In 2017, I was invited by the Hilltop School District to conduct a pilot study of culturally responsive-sustaining education (CRSE) in the systems and practices across the district. Hilltop is a midsize school district located in an East Coast city. The invitation to help Hilltop look at its district from this lens excited me and made me hopeful about the future of learning in this district. Self-inquiry and reflection are the first steps of any transformation process. Because it requires us to expose the things we work so hard to hide as both individuals and organizations, self-reflection is also the hardest and most frightening aspect of change. So it seemed promising that the district voluntarily decided to take this first step toward creating the conditions for change. I integrate some of the findings from the Hilltop pilot study as touchstones throughout the rest of the book.

As a part of the research process, I conducted separate focus groups with students and teachers. All the students and teachers who participated in the focus groups were Black. Both groups were asked to consider the same questions: "How do you feel when you are at school or work?" and "How do you want to feel when you are at school or work?" I asked both groups these questions because of the powerful insights Jackson's (2010) *Pedagogy of Confidence* and Hammond's (2015) *Culturally Responsive Teaching and The Brain* give into the significance of the brain and our nervous systems to learning in general and the importance of CRSE. Learning is an uncertain endeavor saturated with general feelings of stress, anxiety, and fear (Jensen, 2005). For Black students, these feelings are amplified by the daily doses of microaggressions, stress, and disrespect they experience through policies, curricula, relationships, and practices that diminish them. In these environments, Black students are denied the opportunity for authentic and meaningful learning.

The responses of the students and teachers from Hilltop who participated in the focus groups are by no means representative of the feelings or concerns of the district's students or teachers overall. They do, however, provide a glimpse of the possible emotional states these students and teachers experienced in this district's schools and classrooms and how they wanted to feel more of the time. Both groups expressed alarming states of disconnection, stress, anxiety, frustration, and a general lack of emotional safety. Students described feelings of being disrespected and judged. Teachers expressed feeling targeted, torn down, and psychologically unsafe. When students argued that "the curriculum sucks" and "does not prepare them for college," teachers said they could not serve their kids as much as they wanted to. Yet amid these exhausting and diminishing emotions, the students and teachers also expressed intermittent feelings of belonging, pride, purpose, and excitement.

BELONGING

- Student: "Family. What made me make friends and feel accepted was probably the soccer team."
- Teacher: "Like a team. We come in here every day and work together. I don't want to miss a day."

PURPOSE

- Student: "Independent. Everything you do is really up to you. No one is going to make you go to class or tell you to do your homework. It's really what you want."
- Teacher: "I love where I am because I have the liberty to teach, and I am being supported."

PRIDE

- Student: "School pride. At my school, when it comes to sports, all of us get excited, especially when it comes to our basketball and track team."
- Teacher: "Fantastic in the way you are able to enrich students."

Student and teacher responses for how they want to feel at school and work are captured in Table 6.1. The similar feelings expressed by both groups appear in bolded italicized font. Belonging, purpose, and pride emerged as feelings the students and teachers wanted to experience more. They were core to how students and teachers wanted to feel at school and work, as were safety and excitement. There is a shared desire to "matter," or to feel "important" or "significant," which was primarily expressed by both groups in statements made about "respect."

TABLE 6.1 • Table of How Hilltop Students and Teachers Want to Feel When at School and Work

STUDENTS	TEACHERS
I want to feel secure.	***I want to feel safe.***
I want to feel known. They know my name, about my family, my grades.	***Freedom*** to supplement the curriculum with literature with history that reflects the students that I teach, which are predominantly Black and brown and Muslim as well.
I want to feel wanted. I am greeted when I arrive in the building and enter classrooms.	I want to feel like I am ***part of a body of educators and administrators*** who really want to ***have a positive effect*** on our ability to ***make a difference*** in these kids' lives and to ***educate them well***.
I want to feel important.	I want to feel like I don't have to be a part of politics and can still be respected. ***I don't want to feel left out because I don't want to be a part of it***.
I want to feel like I am in a warm setting.	I want to feel like ***my students matter,*** like their struggles mean something to the district.
Like I deserve respect.	***Supported.***
A sense of ***freedom*** to be able ***to express myself.***	***Excited*** to teach.
Like I am smart, and I can do what everyone else can.	***Feel confident that my job was accomplished*** and that what didn't get done today will be done the next day. That my best was put into it.
That being there matters.	***Respect*** the fact that I am doing something right now. Contented.
One-on-one attention and ***support.***	***Significant.***
I want to feel accomplishment. I want to know that I am walking to school for a ***purpose***.	I want to feel ***support*** and ***trust***.
I want to feel ***excited*** to get to college.	
I want to feel like I am around good people.	

Students and teachers alike expressed a sense of freedom as a feeling they want to have when at school and work. Students wanted the freedom to express and be themselves and teachers to provide content that reflects their students. While safety in schools and districts with large Black student populations is generally characterized in terms of safety from physical violence, these students' desire to "be themselves" reiterates research about the importance of school culture and psychological safety to student engagement and learning (Rogers, 2019). Simply put, the Black students in this pilot want to experience belonging and affirmation in their school community.

Responses like, "I want to feel accomplishment," "I want to know that I am walking to school for a purpose," and "One-on-one attention and support" demonstrate the importance of students feeling engaged in meaningful, relevant, and challenging learning in a supportive environment. CRSE tools, like the *Culturally Responsive Curriculum Scorecards* developed by the Metropolitan Center for Urban Education at New York University, identify these experiences as significant to learning (Gooden, Hester, & Peeples, 2019).

Teacher comments centered largely around a desire to be a respected part of an educational community where they can safely meet the needs of students in a supportive environment and to be part of an environment where they and their students matter. The students' comments convey a deep longing for connection, mattering, and meaning in their learning experiences. The following two quotes, one from a student and the other from a teacher, demonstrate that creating educational ecosystems where Black students matter is not negotiable:

Student: "Motivated to feel like myself. I want to feel bigger than what they see me as."

Teacher: "I want to feel like my students matter, like their struggles mean something to the district. Not just to them, and to me but to the whole district."

Insights from Black students in Hilltop show how alienation, toxicity, and stress characterize their learning experiences via the educational survival complex. Black teachers have similar professional experiences. The experiences and feelings both groups identify go beyond the typical emotions accompanying the risk and challenge associated with teaching and learning to more chronic feelings of negation and erasure stemming from the diffusion of anti-Black culture from society to our districts, schools, and classrooms. This disheartening student comment, "Like I am smart, and I can do what everyone else can," illustrates the connection Black students make between their mediocre school experiences and the belief that they are less intelligent than other students in their school. It makes sense that the Hilltop students and teachers want to experience and feel more belonging, pride, purpose, and excitement in the school and classroom environment. These feelings correlate with the bottom tiers of Abraham Maslow's (2013) hierarchy of needs: physiological needs, safety needs, belonging and love needs, and esteem needs. Maslow's hierarchy influenced the widely held view that students cannot perform to their fullest potential if the basic needs of the bottom tiers are not met. The most elemental needs of Black students can never be met in an educational ecosystem that operates from white supremacy and anti-Blackness because these deficit beliefs are oppositional to the basic needs of Black people.

As Central High School demonstrates in Chapter 2, creating classrooms, schools, and districts where Black students and the educators who teach them matter happens on purpose and by design. But in the essay *"Up From the Parched Earth: Toward a Theory of African-American Achievement,"* Perry, Steele, and Hilliard (2003) observe:

> Most schools are simply an assemblage of disconnected activities and events. Almost none have a well-articulated message about the intellectual competence of their students. And if a school does have a message, it is often nothing more than a series of statements made by teachers and principals. Few administrators know how to effectively use the cultural formation of their school's multiracial and multiethnic students to frame a central message, to create a figured community, and to carefully craft a school culture of achievement that has salience for the students.

Emancipatory educational ecosystems that fearlessly empower the potential of Black children require us to name the beliefs that currently operate in our educational ecosystems, eliminate the deficit beliefs that are in operation, and hardwire the belief that Black students matter into the collective unconscious of their school culture. There are no short-cuts or alternate routes. Chapter 7 looks more closely at the relationship between our beliefs and actions and how beliefs operate in our subconscious, and conscious thinking is and provides a brief look at new neuroscience research that is beginning to illuminate specific interactions between culture and our brains.

PAUSE AND PROCESS

Individual Reflection

1. What emotions do you think are important to Black students' learning?
2. What evidence of these emotions have you observed in your educational ecosystem?
3. In what ways does your educational ecosystem inhibit these emotions in student learning?

Collective Planning (in a grade level, department, school, leadership team, parent, community, or other collective meeting space)

Partner with someone in your grade level, content area, school, or at your table. Discuss the emotions you think are important to Black students' learning. What commonalities do you find with your partner? Differences? What do you notice about your shared beliefs? What outlying beliefs do you observe?

Continue to aggregate the exploration of what you have been taught to believe about Black people and other people of color until you culminate with a whole-group discussion about what you collectively notice about your educational ecosystem.

Why You Might Resist Accepting That Anti-Black Culture and Deficit-Beliefs Exist in Your Educational Ecosystem.

1. America's cultural DNA is coded with narratives like "the land of opportunity" and "education is the great equalizer."
2. If anti-Black culture and deficit beliefs are present in our classrooms, schools, and districts, we must acknowledge they are present in us.
3. You are comfortable with the way things are.

Additional Resources

Davis, L. P., & Museus, S. D. (2019). What is deficit thinking? An analysis of conceptualizations of deficit thinking and implications for scholarly research. *NCID Currents, 1*(1). https://doi.org/10.3998/currents.17387731.0001.110

Sealey-Ruiz, Y. (n.d.). Archaeology of self (TM). Retrieved January 26, 2023, from https://www.yolandasealeyruiz.com/archaeology-of-self

White Supremacy Culture. (n.d.). Retrieved January 22, 2023, from https://www.whitesupremacyculture.info/

CHAPTER 7

Beliefs and Biology

Subconscious and Conscious Thinking

Our deep cultural values program our brain on how to interpret the world around us–what a real threat looks like and what will bring a sense of security.

—Zaretta Hammond

A further aspect of beliefs is that they typically become manifest below the level of awareness, as their processing in the nervous system occurs in the range of milliseconds.

—Rüdiger Seitz and Angel Hans-Ferdinand

The culture of a classroom, school, or district is the software that programs every aspect of the learning that occurs within the ecosystem. "Cultures are developed by shared belief in what is determined to be inherently relevant and meaningful to the group" (Jackson, 2010). The shared beliefs held within and across classrooms, schools, and districts form the core of an educational ecosystem's culture. Beliefs are evident in budgets, curriculum maps, policies, schedules, professional learning opportunities, and the display of the artifacts on classroom and school walls. They are communicated through procedures and rules, social media, announcements, assemblies, partnerships, content, and the relationships we develop.

All these components of the learning environment organize our behavior and activities so that the underlying beliefs are reinforced and observable in the culture of the ecosystem. For example, the belief that all students are capable of "high intellectual performance" is observable in the universal integration of gifted education strategies in the content and instruction. The belief that culture is significant to learning is conveyed through a culturally responsive-sustaining education framework and system-wide practices that foster inclusiveness and make students' cultural referents and ways of being central to the design of student learning. Unexamined beliefs about race, culture, gender and gender identity, sexual orientation, learning styles, and socioeconomic status affect how we work with students and families and relate to their communities. This chapter explores how beliefs operate in our thinking to become observable behaviors. It helps us understand the connections between biology and culture in learning and demonstrates the importance of identifying the individual and collective beliefs operating in the cultures of our educational ecosystems (Lee, 2010).

My curiosity about the role of beliefs was set in motion in my twenties when I purchased my first book about Buddhist philosophy, *The Heart of the Buddha: Entering the Tibetan Buddhist Path* (Trungpa & Lief, 2010). I was a young woman searching for resources and methods to help me unpack and address the impact of childhood trauma on my life, particularly my thoughts and behaviors. This book was my introduction to mindfulness and its relationship to our thoughts, emotions, and behaviors in everyday life. A decade later, I read *The Universe in a Single Atom: The Convergence of Science and Spirituality*, in which Gyatso (Dalai Lama, 2010), the fourteenth Dalai Lama, articulates the need for "urgent engagement" between Buddhist philosophy and science, bringing our internal world into conversation with the conditions of the external world. Years later, my sister, a talented elementary school educator, introduced me to Jackson's (2010) *The Pedagogy of Confidence: Inspiring High Intellectual Performance in Urban Schools*, which helped begin to connect the inner world of our beliefs and emotions and neuroscience and learning.

Pedagogy of Confidence gave meaning and language to the many "hunches" and observations I had begun accumulating about the learning opportunities afforded to Black students. Jackson's emphasis on language and its centrality to what we communicate to ourselves, our students, and other educators affirmed the dissonance I felt with the "normed" vocabulary of deficits and failure defining the curricula, policies, trainings, and educational plans associated with Black students and the schools they attend (Jackson, 2010). Because this language locates deficits and weaknesses in Black students and their families, communities, AND

SCHOOLS, it engenders learning conditions that prioritize control, classification, and remediation. Deconstructing and peeling away the false neutrality of terms like "urban," "low-achieving," and "minority," Jackson exposes the negative beliefs animating these and other monikers that "disregard realities" and ascribe inferior status to Black students. "The Pedagogy of Confidence is fearless expectation and support for all students to demonstrate high intellectual performance. It is based on the fearless belief that within all of us resides an untapped reservoir of potential to achieve at high levels" (Jackson, 2010). Mapping the relationship between language, culture, and cognition, *Pedagogy of Confidence* established the neurological basis for affirming beliefs and culturally responsive and sustaining learning.

As many of you will agree, most attempts to situate learning in the lived realities of Black students and center their cultural frames of reference in the learning process are treated as "add-ons" or "window dressing," optional accessories to an already complete curriculum if you will. *Pedagogy of Confidence* directly confronted this diminishing view of the role of culture in student learning by articulating the neurological relationship between culture and learning. In so doing, Jackson demonstrates how societal beliefs and ideologies are underexplored aspects of our ecosystems that have a direct impact on what educators do or don't do in our districts, schools, and classrooms. My spark was ignited, and I wanted to know more. Jackson's clarity about the saliency of beliefs to our self-concepts as educators and students and to the behaviors we adopt in relation to positive and negative beliefs about ourselves and others pushed me to want to learn how beliefs become integrated into our neurological structure.

WHAT ARE BELIEFS?

A belief is an idea one holds as being true, or as Anaya, the young woman working the register in The Yard, a local burger spot where I started this chapter, shared with me, "A belief is to have faith that something is true." The exact meaning of "belief" has been explored and studied widely across disciplines and fields. Centuries of debate among philosophers, psychologists, and more recently, epigeneticists who explore the nature of beliefs have not established a precise definition. Nevertheless, belief is a central concept in our lives that connects our internal and external worlds. Beliefs are a part of the language in which our thoughts make meaning of the world. "To be a human thinker or rational agent is, in part, to regard the world and the things in it as having certain features. Believing is just this aspect of being a thinker or agent" (Schwitzgebel, 2011). Beliefs are groups of thought patterns that, when thought repeatedly over time and assigned value, become consistent ways of thinking. Embedded in the very fabric of our language, beliefs organize information and inform our behaviors.

Everyone has beliefs about everything in life. Love, work, politics, money, food, exercise, time, and, of course, education. When you believe in something, you hold a mental attitude of favor toward a proposition or idea that you mentally assert or judge as true (Campbell, 1967). While beliefs are part of both our individual thinking and our collective unconscious, they are not necessarily representations of what is true or factual. Some belief statements like "I believe I can fly" and "If you believe it, you can achieve it" are positive belief statements that we use colloquially to give ourselves a more expansive view of our individual capacity. These beliefs support our self-esteem and help us succeed. Other belief statements, such as "education is the key to success" and "hard work pays off," communicate ideas about important features of our society. Positive beliefs provide the cognitive architecture for us to behave and act in ways that are supportive, mobilizing, caring, and empowering. Negative beliefs, on the other hand, are immobilizing, destructive, and limiting. They cause antipathy or apathy, evoke anger or fear, and affect our emotions in harmful ways.

We all hold and act on beliefs. Our behaviors and actions are filtered through the beliefs we have acquired from various sources since conception. We develop beliefs from events in our lives and interactions with different people as children. Comments about the world and groups of people absorbed from television, overheard in adult conversations, or spoken directly to us also shape our beliefs. Who we observe our families, teachers, or friends interacting (or not interacting) with and the places we were allowed and not allowed to go also exert influence on the beliefs we develop. Beliefs are transmitted and developed through these interactions as they occur at different levels of our ecosystems. The thoughts we have and repeat in our minds in relation to the contextual factors in our lives develop into beliefs, which then act as the filters through which we perceive, understand, and respond to information in our environment (Lee, 2008). They command the brain, which signals our body what to do. Beliefs carry high emotional charges that, as stated previously, can either be positive or negative. The biochemical processes activated by our emotions transmit hormones and neurotransmitters to every cell in the body, making each one of our cells susceptible to our thoughts and beliefs, even those beliefs about which we are consciously unaware. As a result, everything we can observe, or more precisely what we interpret about what we observe, about ourselves and others is the external projection of our conscious and unconscious belief systems onto our material world. From the opposite end of the process, what we think, say, and do provides a window into what we believe.

PAUSE AND PROCESS

Individual Reflection

1. Identify a positive belief you have about yourself as an educator.
   a. What behaviors and/or activities can you identify in your life that confirm you believe this about yourself?
   b. How does this belief assist and support your practice?
2. Identify a deficit belief you have about yourself as an educator.
   a. What behaviors and/or activities can you identify in your life that confirm you believe this about yourself?
   b. How does this belief inhibit your practice?

Collective Planning (in a grade-level, department, school, leadership team, parent, community, or other collective meeting space)

Partner with someone in your grade level, content area, school, or at your table. Discuss the beliefs you have about yourself as an educator. What commonalities do you find with your partner? Differences? What do you notice about your shared beliefs? What outlying beliefs do you observe?

Continue to aggregate the exploration of what you have been taught to believe about Black people and other people of color until you culminate with a whole-group discussion about what you collectively notice about your shared beliefs about yourselves as educators.

HOW BELIEFS OPERATE IN OUR THOUGHTS, FEELINGS, AND BEHAVIORS

The information I share in this chapter about how beliefs are integrated and work in our subconscious, and conscious thinking was acquired through reading cutting-edge research about beliefs and emotions, piecing together various findings that would help me communicate my thinking most effectively, and even spending countless hours of Google searches that brought me to unexpected sources. I found exploring how beliefs become a part of the organization of our thinking important because far too often in school and district meetings and professional development, I have heard the sentiments, "It doesn't matter what I believe: I can still teach" or "I don't care what you believe: This what we do in this school" expressed. The fact is beliefs do matter, and what we actually do says more about what we believe than what we may say we believe.

The cognitive triangle used extensively in therapeutic practices is a useful tool for explicating the connection between what we think, feel, and do. Cognitive models of psychology are based on the "view that knowledge is determined partly by the structure of thinking—or the categories of thought through which we experience 'external reality'" (see Figure 7.1; Leahey & Martell, 2021). Put another way, how we think, how we feel, and how we act all work together.

FIGURE 7.1

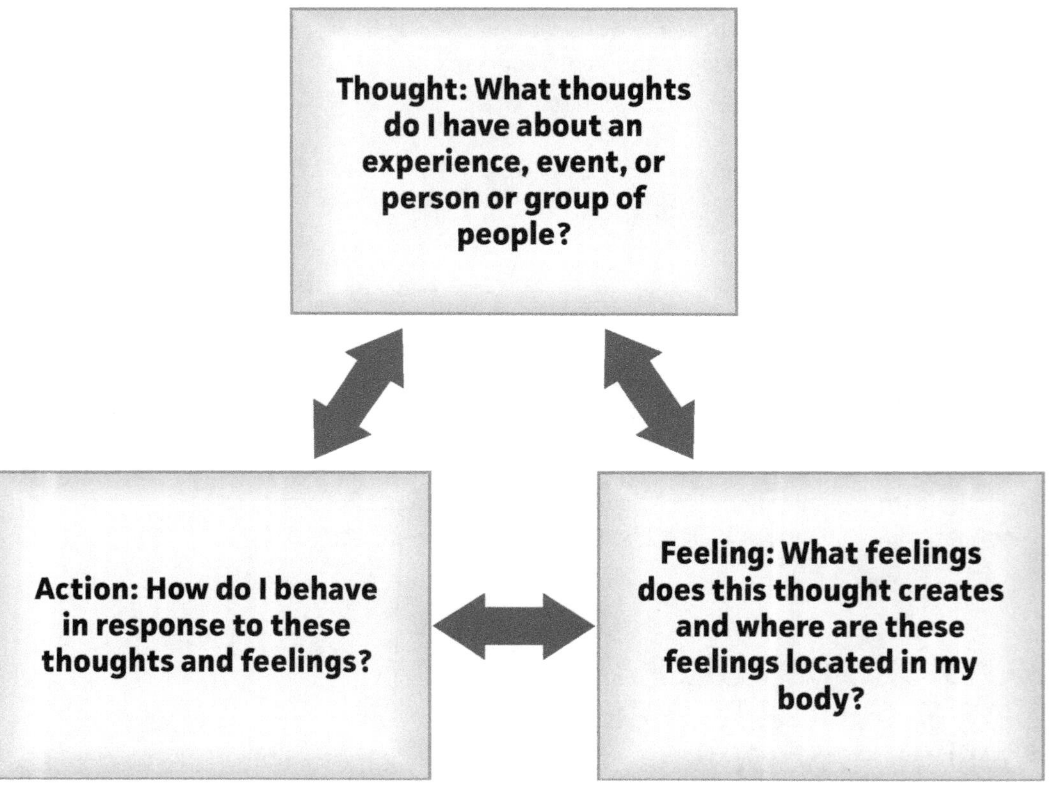

Underlying beliefs shape *how we think* (our perceptions and interpretations) *about* ideas, experiences, events, and people. How we think about an event or person, for example, generates the emotional responses we have in our bodies, which determine *how we feel about* the event or person. *How we act* in response to an event and person is driven, in large part, by how we feel, particularly when we are in environments where our survival instinct is activated (Seitz, 2022). Belief formation is a part of the information processing that takes place in the brain of every student and educator and influences the thoughts, feelings, and actions that occur in our educational ecosystems. Beliefs are also formed and held collectively within and across our educational ecosystems. In Chapter 6, I discussed how deficit beliefs shape the limited learning opportunities and experiences provided to Black students in our classrooms and schools. The cognitive triangle in Figure 7.2 is an example of how deficit thoughts about Black students catalyze feelings and behaviors that produce limited learning experiences for them.

FIGURE 7.2 •

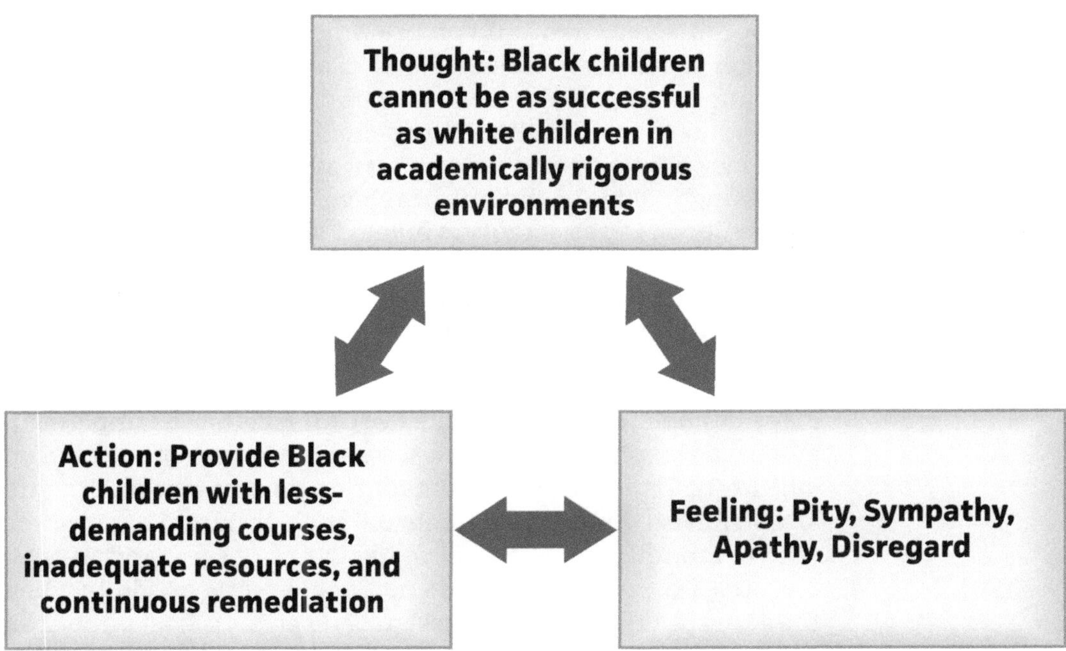

Neuroscientists suggest that beliefs evolved as a part of how we think to help us effectively and efficiently solve problems, navigate our environment, and make decisions by assigning meaning and value to objects in social and physical environments. "Beliefs are the neuropsychic product of neural processes allowing individuals to develop a personal affective stance concerning the signals in their environment" (Seitz & Angel, 2020). Cognitively, beliefs influence both our perceptions and predictions about the people, events, ideas, and experiences in our lives. Beliefs are developed through fundamental brain processes that process and interpret information and send messages to the body through the nervous system.

Author and educator, Zaretta Hammond (2015), whose work I reference throughout this book, refers to the brain's physical structures as the brain's "hardware." Our brain's hardware operates primarily on two seemingly separate levels, conscious and subconscious. The conscious level includes all the mental processes of which we are aware—for example, memories, identity, whether or not you are thirsty or tired, or thoughts you have at any given moment. Solving problems, setting goals for the future, and creating are the business of the conscious level. Automatic mental processes that influence judgments, feelings, and behavior make up the subconscious level. Routine behaviors become automatic and programmed into our subconscious through repetition. We learn to stop at red lights through the on-going conditioning we experience crossing streets as pedestrians and riding in vehicles. In school, we learn to stay to the right by walking up and down stairways and through hallways on the right side. At the physical level, an often-stated example of subconscious activity is breathing. Breathing is a physical process that is regulated involuntarily. When we are anxious, angry, or excited, our breathing accelerates without us consciously telling the respiratory system to do so.

We also have automatic responses that are determined by our cultures and the beliefs we hold. Eye contact is one example of an automatic response that varies across cultural groups. American culture tends to view eye contact as a sign of confidence and attentiveness. American parents tell their children, "Look at me when I am talking to you." In many Latino, Asian, and African cultures, however, children do not look directly at adults when they are speaking to them as a sign of respect. In Black American culture, making eye contact with other Black people is a cultural behavior that is exhibited to recognize each other in various social contexts, particularly those where we are few in number. Making eye contact essentially says, "I see you." This cultural behavior demonstrates the belief that being seen matters.

CULTURE: CONSCIOUS AND SUBCONSCIOUS, OBSERVABLE AND UNOBSERVABLE

Recall Hammond's culture tree from Chapter 6. The surface aspects of culture are represented by the leaves of the tree. The unknown but knowable features of shallow culture are identified in the tree's trunk. Deep culture is located far below the surface in the tree's roots. Culture has also been widely represented by the iceberg. Surface culture is found in the tip of the iceberg, shallow culture is just below the surface of the water, and deep culture lies deep in the water. Non-verbal communication, such as making eye contact (an example of shallow culture) and decision-making (an example of deep culture), are learned behaviors we acquire through continuous exposure to the expectations, values, and behaviors we absorb in our social environment. Like decision-making, beliefs are part of the subconscious aspects of culture that exist below the surface of the tree and iceberg (see Figure 7.3). These two visual models articulate a clear relationship between culture and our subconscious and correspondingly between our beliefs and our observable behaviors.

Hammond's culture tree provides a more dynamic lens into this relationship. Each part of a tree plays multiple, critical roles and exists as part of the overall ecosystem of the tree. No part can work without the others. The leaves on Hammond's culture tree represent the observable elements of surface culture, including food, stories, talk systems, and music. Like the leaves on a tree, these aspects of surface culture nurture and sustain a culture through important rituals—such as recognition and celebration. However, just like the iceberg, these evident features of culture are shaped and influenced by the shallow and deep culture that is transported to leaves through the tree's branches, trunk, and roots. The roots anchor the tree and connect the tree to other trees through an underground root network that communicates and shares the beliefs, attitudes, understandings, and ethics that shape our responses, reactions, and awareness to ourselves and others. The tree trunk facilitates the movement of the elements of deep culture, such as decision-making and worldview, up from the roots in the soil to the branches and, eventually, to the leaves. The trunk also facilitates the reinforcement and dispersion of culture down from the leaves, branches, and trunk back to the roots.

Ultimately, both models underscore the analogous relationship between our conscious and subconscious thinking and the observable and unobservable aspects of culture and beliefs. Surface culture exists in our conscious minds and is exhibited deliberately based on established cultural knowledge and expectations. Deep culture is embedded in our subconscious minds and is communicated to our conscious minds through the patterns of thinking and behaving we have developed over the course of our lives through exposure and experience. Deep culture is the primary program running through the hardware of our brain. As a result, when we observe and assess the visible and tangible aspects of cultures outside of our own, we do so based on the features of our own deep culture, which unless actively brought to our consciousness through reflection about ourselves and cultures, remains inaccessible to us.

FIGURE 7.3

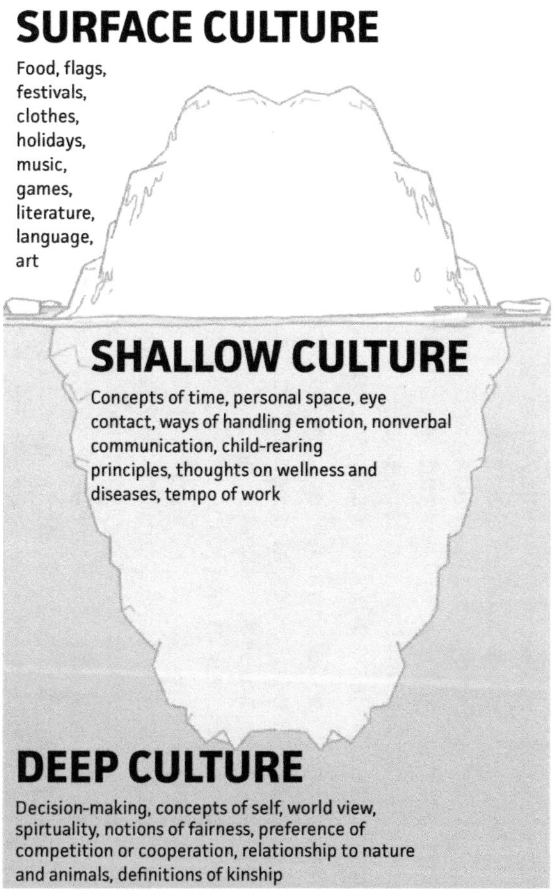

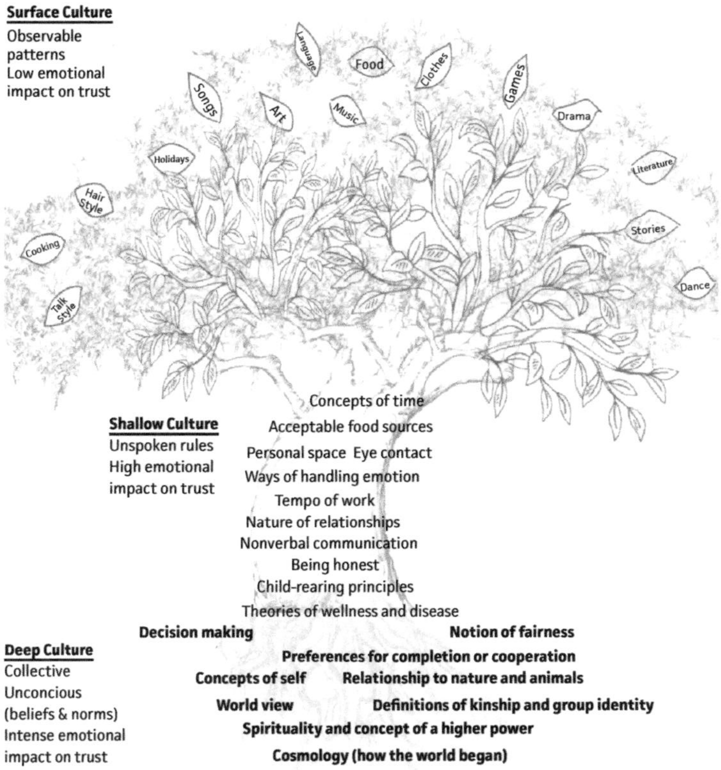

SURFACE CULTURE

Food, flags, festivals, clothes, holidays, music, games, literature, language, art

SHALLOW CULTURE

Concepts of time, personal space, eye contact, ways of handling emotion, nonverbal communication, child-rearing principles, thoughts on wellness and diseases, tempo of work

DEEP CULTURE

Decision-making, concepts of self, world view, spirituality, notions of fairness, preference of competition or cooperation, relationship to nature and animals, definitions of kinship

Surface Culture
Observable patterns
Low emotional impact on trust

Language
Food
Clothes
Games
Songs
Art
Music
Drama
Holidays
Literature
Hair Style
Stories
Cooking
Dance
Talk Style

Shallow Culture
Unspoken rules
High emotional impact on trust

Concepts of time
Acceptable food sources
Personal space Eye contact
Ways of handling emotion
Tempo of work
Nature of relationships
Nonverbal communication
Being honest
Child-rearing principles
Theories of wellness and disease

Deep Culture
Collective
Unconcious
(beliefs & norms)
Intense emotional impact on trust

Decision making
Notion of fairness
Preferences for completion or cooperation
Concepts of self
Relationship to nature and animals
World view
Definitions of kinship and group identity
Spirituality and concept of a higher power
Cosmology (how the world began)

Content adapted from Hammond, Z. (2015). Graphics by Eion Haynes.

Our brains are designed to assess and process information in the environment around us. We process information through our cultural frames of reference (Jackson, 2010; Hammond, 2015). The subconscious operates like a security system, continuously scanning to detect internal and external threats to our safety and well-being. Because the subconscious detects and monitors danger and risks, it springs into action without guidance or direction from us whenever harm seems imminent. Harm could be anticipated from the irritation of mosquitoes buzzing in your ear or a microaggression—such as "Your Black students are all continuously doing worse than the rest of the students in the school" being said to the Black teachers in a staff meeting. The subconscious may also signal danger in the scowl on someone's face when you enter an elevator or when a discussion of data at a professional development session focuses on addressing weakness as the solution to the so-called "achievement gap." The subconscious also goes full throttle because of unacknowledged negative beliefs we hold about ourselves, a group of people, or a social situation, even when these beliefs are experientially unfounded or derived from historically or socially inaccurate information and data. This is because our beliefs are stored in our reptilian brain, the oldest part of our brain that is designed to literally survive hostile environments, and our limbic system, which integrates our emotions, cognition, and behavior in this system.

Coming full circle to where this chapter began, our beliefs are developed through our ongoing and continuous interaction with our environment, which are shaped and determined by our cultural context and ultimately stored in our subconscious. As long as the beliefs we carry remain unquestioned and unknown to us, they operate automatically, filtering into our behaviors and actions via the roots and trunk of the tree to become the visible leaves we display through our engagement with life. Our conscious mind, on the other hand, works to use new information to evaluate our environment and experiences. When we are awake, both systems are always operating. They don't function in isolation but instead operate in a precise and coordinated feedback loop that allows for the continuous processing of internal and external information. However, using our conscious mind to establish new beliefs and new ways of thinking and believing requires that we identify the beliefs, thoughts, feelings, and behaviors that are already activated in our subconscious. For example, "Black children are less well-behaved than white children" is a belief that operates automatically via the "educational survival complex" in most classrooms, schools, and districts. This belief drives thoughts such as "Black boys need to be disciplined more frequently and harshly," which create feelings such as anger and control as opposed to care and empowerment and lead to discipline policies and practices that remove Black boys from classrooms and schools and increase their interaction with law enforcement. Whether examining school, district, state, or national data about the rates and methods for disciplining Black boys, disproportionality analysis bears out predictable patterns in the referrals and suspensions for Black boys. This belief creates a culture of punishment that perniciously targets Black children and is symbolic of the educational survival complex.

PAUSE AND PROCESS

Individual Reflection

1. Identify a positive belief about Black students operating in your educational ecosystem.
   a. What behaviors and/or activities can you identify in your life that confirm that this belief operates in your educational ecosystem?
   b. How does this belief assist and support your educational ecosystem?
   c. What does your data tell you?
2. Identify a deficit belief about Black students operating in your educational ecosystem.
   a. What behaviors and/or activities can you identify in your life that confirm that this belief operates in your educational ecosystem?
   b. How does this belief inhibit your educational ecosystem?
   c. What does your data tell you?

Collective Planning (in a grade level, department, school, leadership team, parent, community, or other collective meeting space)

Partner with someone in your grade level, content area, school, or at your table. Discuss the beliefs about Black students operating in your educational ecosystem. What commonalities do you find with your partner? Differences? What do you notice about your shared beliefs? What outlying beliefs do you observe?

Continue to aggregate the exploration of the beliefs about Black students operating in your educational ecosystem until you culminate with a whole-group discussion about what you collectively notice about your beliefs about yourselves as educators.

WHAT WE CAN LEARN FROM STUDYING OUR BRAINS

Study of the brain structures related to the processes of believing has been made possible due to advances in neuroscience research. For example, functional MRI studies, which evaluate which areas of the brain are involved in certain functions, such as speech and vision, have also been applied to the study of belief formation. Rüdiger Seitz and Hans-Ferdinand Angel, a team of researchers from universities in Austria and Germany, have identified the sensory domains involving reinforcement learning as the location in the brain where beliefs appear to form (Seitz & Angel, 2020). Beliefs and believing may involve multiple mental operations that support perception, valuation, information storage, and prediction (Seitz, 2022). Further research suggests that there are differences in neural processing that exist across cultures. "Development of culturally specific beliefs and belief processes may be understood from the perspective of the culture–behavior–brain loop model of human development, which suggests both indirect culture–brain interactions, through the practice of behaviors, and direct culture–brain interactions, which constitute an interacting loop that provides a basis of human development. Shared beliefs provide a bridge to link social behavior and the brain and guide their interactions in a specific socio-cultural environment, which in turn results in the development of distinct neurocognitive processes underlying belief" (Han, 2022). Not only are the beliefs we hold deeply integrated into our neurocognitive structure, but they are activated through distinct neurocognitive processes that may vary across cultures.

I find the knowledge being generated from this research so empowering to our work as educators. First, it confirms that our beliefs develop through the information we receive in different sociocultural environments, or what we can think of as our cultural frames of reference. Second, it gives us a window into how the beliefs we hold are mobilized by the interactions of the "hardware" located in both our subconscious and conscious minds, providing insights into the neurobiology of beliefs. To understand these processes and the different roles of the hardware in our subconscious and conscious minds, we will briefly consider several key aspects of the brain's physical structure as they relate specifically to belief formation and processing.

NEURONS, NEUROGLIA, AND THE MYELIN SHEATH

There are over 100 billion neurons in each of our brains, and we continue to generate new neurons in different parts of our brains throughout our lifetimes. Neurons are the information transmitters of our nervous system. They transmit information between different areas of the brain and between the brain and the rest of the nervous system using electrical impulses and chemical signals. Neurons make everything we think, feel, and do possible (see Figure 7.4).

FIGURE 7.4 ● Diagram of a Neuron

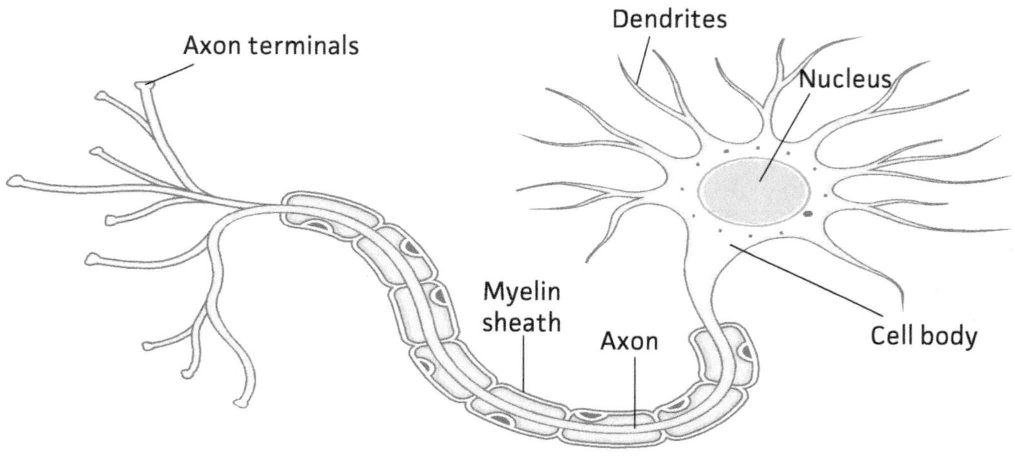

Image by https://www.istockphoto.com/portfolio/L.Darin

Neural networks form when neurons communicate repeatedly as we repeat or practice the same action over and over. Repetition increases the myelin sheath, which is responsible for transmitting the electrical impulses across cells and networks, leading to faster and more efficient processing of the cell signals—and better performance. Repetition through our family upbringings, social interactions, educational experiences, and exposure to cultural ideas is core to the development of the neural networks that structure beliefs in our brains.

REGIONS OF THE BRAIN AND BELIEF FORMATION: SUBCONSCIOUS AND CONSCIOUS THINKING

The weight of the brain increases from birth through adulthood, when it becomes approximately the size of a three-pound grapefruit. The folds in the brain give it the textured appearance of a walnut. Our brains are composed mostly of water, fat, and proteins. Though I can bring to mind numerous quips and sayings that suggest the brain is mostly fat or a muscle, neither is true. The brain is, in fact, mostly water. It also contains blood vessels and nerves, including neurons and neuroglia. The brain and the spinal cord form our central nervous system, which combines information from the entire body and coordinates activity across the whole organism. The intricate network of systems, cells, and nerves that make up our brains is designed to detect anything threatening. Our brain has evolved throughout the course of human history, refining its architecture and systems so that we are able to process increasingly complex information and respond to our environment in ways that ensure our survival.

The walnut-like folds of our brains are divided into four different regions called lobes: frontal, parietal, temporal, and occipital. Subconscious and conscious thinking operate across these regions to carry out the various functions of our nervous system. Beliefs are formed through the communication of the brain's systems across different regions and communicated to our bodies by these systems working in unison with the nervous system. "Distinct beliefs not only influence people's behaviors but also shape how their brains work" (Han, 2022).

SUBCONSCIOUS

The subconscious detects and goes on high alert whenever negative beliefs drive our thinking, whether that thinking is about ourselves, others, or the experiences, situations, or conditions we face (Sugiura et al., 2015):

- The reticular activating system, or RAS, is activated and filters negative beliefs so that your brain pays attention and looks for confirmation of the negative beliefs in your external environment. The RAS determines what incoming information is relevant to these beliefs and only allows the most pertinent information through.

- The thalamus communicates to different parts of the brain, activating widespread circuits that allow us to filter incoming information through our beliefs to make attributions, assign emotions to our thoughts and experiences, and determine how we will express our ideas about any present event or experience. These circuits help us make predictions about future events or experiences based on our beliefs.

CONSCIOUS

Areas of our brain that have been reported to be critical to the "valuation of sensory information" (Seitz et al., 2009) and schema that "generalize across different stories, subjects, and modalities" support our conscious thinking (Baldassamo et al., 2018):

- The cerebral cortex is responsible for higher-level thinking and processing, such as reasoning, evaluation, emotion, and decision-making in our brains. Research indicates the neural representations for beliefs or the coding that represents and makes decisions about how to respond to beliefs, may be stored in the cerebral cortex (Seitz, 2022).

For at least the last seven decades, education reform has failed to realize that because change begins with our thinking and is explicitly linked to the beliefs we hold as individuals and as a society about what education is as well as about different groups of students, technical reforms alone are insufficient and consistently lead to the same outcomes. Creating schools and classrooms where Black children have the opportunity to experience and use the depths of their intellect requires we challenge the anti-Black culture that powers deficit beliefs within our educational ecosystems. Just as neuroplasticity has shown us the human brain can be rewired to eliminate harmful and negative patterns in the brain, we must begin to think about education transformation as rewiring schools to untether them and us from the toxic cultures and beliefs that the educational survival complex produces within them. Chapter 8 shares affirming beliefs that can help you move closer to emancipatory educational ecosystems where learning is connected to the identities, cultures, histories, and communities of Black students.

Why You Might Resist Accepting That Beliefs Program Our Thinking

1. The idea that beliefs are hardwired into our thinking through complex cognitive processes is very scientific and you aren't "good" at science.
2. Focusing on the external world is easier than investigating our internal worlds, individually or collectively.
3. Acknowledging that beliefs impact everything we do makes us responsible for everything we do.

Additional Resources

Culturally Responsive Teaching & the Brain. (2020, June 23). Retrieved January 22, 2023, from https://crtandthebrain.com/

The Pedagogy of Confidence Homepage. (n.d.). Retrieved January 22, 2023, from https://pedagogyofconfidence.net/the-pedagogy-of-confidence/

PART III

Collective Purpose

The chapters in this section support the development of collective purpose. Collective purpose is what we create through engaging in conscious collectivism. It is the collective agreement to work together to eliminate white supremacy and anti-Blackness in our educational ecosystems and to intentionally move toward emancipatory educational ecosystems that affirm Black students. These chapters introduce affirming beliefs and demonstrate the importance of CRSET to the collective purpose of an emancipatory educational ecosystem.

CHAPTER 8

Affirming Beliefs That Transform Learning

We must imagine new worlds that transition ideologies and norms, so that no one sees Black people as murderers, or Brown people as terrorists and aliens, but all of us as potential cultural and economic innovators.

—adrienne maree brown

These beliefs were ground up and served as grits, communicated with the regularity of a mother's prayers, like a drumbeat, a mission.

—Theresa Perry

In Chapter 7, I explored and defined beliefs and examined how beliefs are developed and structured in our subconscious and conscious thinking, including the role of beliefs in shaping how we interpret, understand, and interact with the world around us. Chapter 7 also laid a foundation for understanding how the shared beliefs of our educational ecosystems operate within these systems. Now that we have begun to develop a shared understanding in these areas, it is time to move into more proactive thinking about the beliefs that can be generative of emancipatory educational ecosystems. In this chapter, I introduce affirming beliefs that can help disrupt the deficit beliefs that diminish and harm Black students: Black lives matter; belonging; interdependence; and empowerment. Working synergistically like the principles in the ecosystems that exist around us, these beliefs can empower emancipatory educational ecosystems to intentionally see and tap into the interests, talents, and gifts of the Black students who are waiting for us to see them.

Emancipatory educational ecosystems cannot be created from familiar levels of believing, thinking, and doing. To create a new paradigm for our students, the ability to think and act at the level of this vision must be developed. For the most part, the work of educators has been constructed on the beliefs and practices of an anti-Black, deficit-based education system. For most, functioning from these beliefs is automatic and accepted. However, to move toward imagining educational ecosystems where Black children are educated to their fullest potential, these toxic and limiting deficit beliefs must be supplanted by beliefs that are affirming, restorative, and limitless.

Howard Washington Thurman, a theologian and activist who played a leading role in many social justice movements and organizations and was a mentor to Dr. King, said, "You are the only you that has ever lived; your idiom [your unique signature] is the only idiom of its kind in all of existence and if you cannot hear the sound of the genuine in you, you will all of your life spend your days on the ends of strings that somebody else pulls" (Thurman, 1980). In the sections that follow, I share beliefs that will help us imagine the emancipatory educational ecosystems that can uncover "the sound of the genuine" in ourselves and our Black students (see Figure 8.1):

- Black lives matter
- Belonging
- Interdependence
- Empowerment

The beliefs discussed in this chapter support four key shifts in educational ecosystems: (1) shifting the beliefs educators have of Black students and Black communities; (2) shifting Black students' beliefs about themselves, their culture, and communities; (3) shifting the beliefs all students have about each other; and (4) shifting educators' beliefs about their capacity for change. Table 8.1 picks up on the work of Edward Fergus and highlights a few of these shifts.

FIGURE 8.1 •

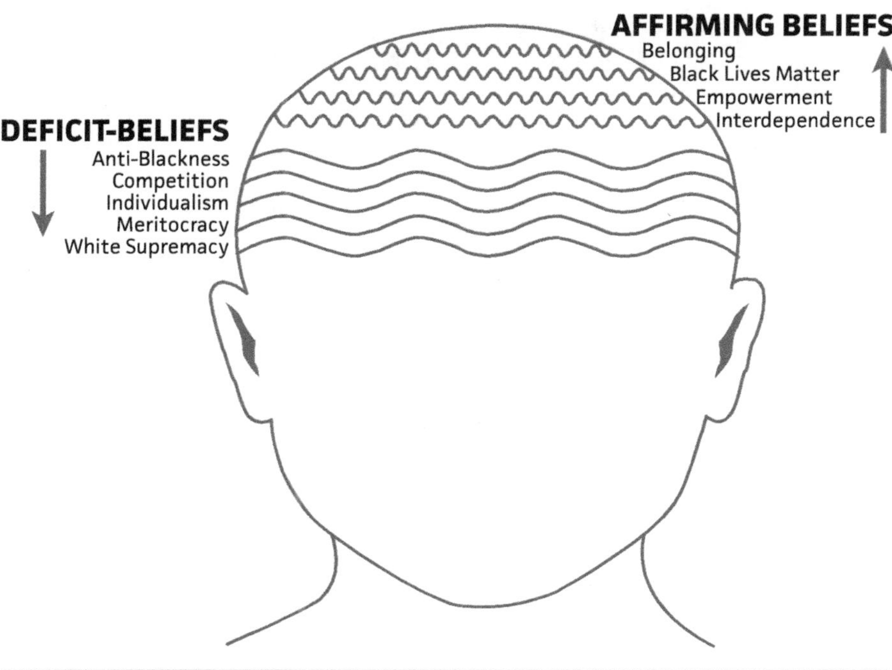

TABLE 8.1 • Choosing Affirming Beliefs Over Deficit Beliefs

DEFICIT-BASED THOUGHTS (FERGUS, 2017)	AFFIRMING UNDERSTANDINGS
Students of color from disadvantaged homes just seem to show a lack of interest.	Curriculum and classroom instruction that are congruent with the cultures and representative of the histories of Black students elicit their interest.
Disadvantaged students generally do not have the abilities necessary to succeed in the classroom.	Black students are successful in classrooms, schools, and districts where an architecture of support structures is in place to support their learning styles and needs.
Students from disadvantaged backgrounds do not value education as much as other students.	Black students value education that values them.
It is important that students of color assimilate so that they can succeed in mainstream culture.	The more that the cultural frames of reference, assets, and histories of Black students are valued in their education, the more successful they will be.

(Continued)

(Continued)

DEFICIT-BASED THOUGHTS (FERGUS, 2017)	AFFIRMING UNDERSTANDINGS
Unfortunately, for many people of color, education is just not a real priority.	Black people have pursued education to improve their conditions even when the quality of education afforded to them did not support their success.
Schools cannot be expected to overcome the disadvantages of race and poverty.	Schools that operate as part of their larger ecosystem can connect to resources and opportunities that support students and families to address basic needs.
There is not so much schools can do to close the achievement gap.	When schools and districts build the awareness, knowledge, and skills of their ecosystems to understand individual, institutional, and structural racism, they can address "opportunity gaps."
Trying to be culturally responsive all of the time is a nice theory, but the reality is that a teacher does not have time to be all things to all students.	All teachers can build relationships with Black students, elicit their cultural knowledge, validate their prior experiences, and amplify their voices in learning to make it responsive and effective for them.
Although I am hesitant to say it publicly, I believe that racial difference in intelligence may have a hereditary or genetic component.	Race is social construct and has nothing to do with the distribution of characteristics that exist among all people.

BLACK LIVES MATTER

In 2013, after George Zimmerman was acquitted for the murder of Trayvon Martin, three Black women—Alicia Garza, Patrisse Khan-Cullors, and Opal Tometi—ignited the hashtag #blacklivesmatter on Twitter. Alicia tweeted first, "Black people. I love you. I love us. Our lives matter." Patrisse responded, "declaration: black bodies will no longer be sacrificed for the rest of the world's enlightenment. i am done. i am so done. trayvon you are loved infinitely #blacklivesmatter." These tweets have since catalyzed on-going public dialogue, organization, and mobilization to address "the state-sanctioned violence" experienced by Black people across the country (Black Lives Matter [BLM], 2021). The Black Lives Matter at School movement, which began on October 19th, 2016, with 1,000 Seattle educators arriving at school wearing T-shirts that read "Black Lives Matter: We Stand Together," unites educators, parents, students, and communities in "a new phase of long struggle to transform the conditions of teaching and learning for Black students in this country (Jones & Hagopian, 2020). As a belief, Black lives matter is the unambiguous belief in the humanity, dignity, intelligence, beauty, and worth of Black people to our society and the entire planet, that Black people, Black history, Black culture(s), Black experiences, and Black sensibilities are vital to the past, present, and future, and Black people have the right to be everywhere and be vibrantly, joyfully, creatively, largely, and abundantly *alive* wherever we are.

Working from the mindset that Black lives matter refocuses attention on creating learning conditions where this belief is the active current in our culture, systems, policies, procedures, curriculum, and strategies. It moves through classrooms, schools, or districts like electrons through a wire to generate electricity. The learning environment, the relationships formed there, how learning and teaching are designed, the nature of discipline, and the connection of the ecosystem to the community become hardwired to value the historical and lived experiences of our Black students. Culture becomes centralized in everything we do. Everything about our students, no matter how far removed our personal experiences or context, becomes the platform for learning. Black students are invited to see their value and use what they bring with them to schools and classrooms to boldly and creatively own their learning, strengthen their identities, and sustain their culture(s).

When our goal is to create affirming and sustaining learning experiences for Black students, we are able to envision classrooms, schools, and districts where Black students are

- immersed in cultures of love and care,
- nourished by curricula and content that affirms their value to the world,
- engaged through instructional strategies that draw out their talents, interests, and gifts,
- assessed through measures designed to make meaning of their learning, and
- supported with interventions that promote wholeness and healing.

Without the conscious and purposeful re-habituation of your thinking and actions to the belief that Black lives matter, the cultures, policies, and practices that result from anti-Black deficit thinking will continue to be reproduced. As a belief, Black lives matter takes you to the affirming and culturally centered view needed to help you move toward new paradigms for schools and learning for Black students. If you truly want to create classrooms, schools, and districts where Black children learn at the precipice of their brilliance and joy because they are Black and not despite it, then believing that Black lives matter is not negotiable.

PAUSE AND PROCESS

Individual Reflection

Find a quiet place to practice observing your thinking. Once you are comfortable, reflect on these questions:

1. What does Black lives matter mean to you?
2. Read the belief "Black lives matter" out loud several times. As you read, notice your physical responses.
   - Are there parts of the belief statement that follow that make you feel uncomfortable or tense?
   - Are there parts of the belief statement that make you feel a sense of gratification or affinity?
   - What do the feelings and sensations you experience tell you about how you currently relate to this belief?

   "Black lives matter is the unambiguous belief in the humanity, dignity, intelligence, beauty, and worth of Black people to our society and the planet. It is the belief that Black people, Black history, Black culture(s), Black experiences, and Black sensibilities are vital to the past, present, and future branches of the human family. It is the belief that Black people have the right to be everywhere and be vibrantly, joyfully, creatively, largely, and abundantly alive wherever we are."

Collective Planning (in a grade level, department, school, leadership team, parent, community, or other collective meeting space)

Partner with someone in your grade level, content area, school, or at your table. Discuss your reactions to the belief Black lives matter. What commonalities do you find with your partner? Differences? What do you notice about your shared reactions? What outlying reactions do you observe?

Continue to aggregate the exploration of your reactions to the belief Black lives matter until you culminate with a whole-group discussion about what you collectively notice about your shared reactions to the belief Black lives matter.

BELONGING

Students learn and develop in and through relationships with others and the world around them. Students' development is a socially mediated process in which cultural values, beliefs, and problem-solving strategies are acquired through collaborative dialogues with someone who can engage them slightly beyond what they already know and can do. This sociocultural understanding of learning, articulated by Lev Vygotsky, includes concepts such as culture-specific tools, private speech, and the zone of proximal development (ZPD). The ZPD is "the space between what a learner can do without assistance and what a learner can do with adult guidance or in collaboration with more capable peers" (Vygotsky et al., 1978). The ZPD is where prior knowledge interacts with new knowledge, where new neural networks are formed, and where learning happens. It is the place where you can see, hear, and feel students making connections and applying their knowledge. Every aspect of educators' work is geared toward engendering the conditions for this sweet spot to unfold in our classrooms, schools, and districts. Yet no one can cross the threshold into this sacred space if the door does not open with an invitation of belonging.

Researcher and author Brené Brown and poet Najwa Zebian have both influenced my understanding of what belonging is and how to more thoughtfully nurture belonging in my work with educators and communities. Both of their explorations of belonging teach that, while belonging is often viewed as "fitting in," it is less about our relationships with other people and more about how we relate to ourselves so we can show up wherever we are as our authentic selves. In *Braving the Wilderness: The Question for True Belonging and Standing Alone*, Brown (2019) defines "true belonging" as "the spiritual practice of believing in and belonging to yourself so deeply that you can share your most authentic self with the world and find sacredness in both being a part of something and standing alone in the wilderness." Belonging is the surest sense of safety and security about who one is so that we can bring our full selves to interact with everyone we encounter and everything we do.

Being seen and accepted is a basic need that must be met for any of us to take the risks associated with learning. The learning process involves demonstrating what you already know about a topic as well as acquiring new information or skills. Students' knowledge and skills are observed, measured, evaluated, and compared. Students' mistakes, incorrect answers, attempts to "get it," doubts, insecurities, and frustrations all come to the surface and are subject to feedback. Learning requires that students expose their thinking and other parts of their inner world to us and trust us with it. They are inherently vulnerable as learners. Educators are also vulnerable, as our intellect and competency are visible aspects of our work that are routinely evaluated.

The stakes attached to being vulnerable are particularly high for Black students whose knowledge, experiences, skills, dispositions, and behaviors are routinely viewed as irrelevant and unimportant to the acquisition of "academic knowledge." In this context, rejection, erasure, and self-abnegation are embedded in the learning experiences of Black students, which makes engaging in learning unsafe for them cognitively, emotionally, and spiritually. Black students are continuously required to make choices about the pieces of themselves that they carry with them in our classrooms, schools, and districts. Where connection and relationship should be nurtured, alienation and separation are instead normalized. The door to the ZPD is not available to Black students if it does not lead to a sanctuary where they are welcomed to enter exactly as they are.

It is our responsibility to make classrooms, schools, and districts spaces where Black students are welcomed, loved, supported, and engaged as they are and to do so with the intention of fortifying their understanding that "(their) existence—who and how (they) are—is in and of itself a contribution to the people and place around (them)" (Brown, 2019). Designing classroom and other learning experiences where students are enabled to uncover what they know and put that knowledge into conversation and interaction with new ideas, concepts, and perspectives is one aspect of this shift. Connection and relationship are, of course, elemental to fostering such deep engagement in learning where students feel secure in themselves and safe with us. The cultivation of this "true belonging" in our educational ecosystems rests on strengthening the relationships students have with themselves as well as the bonds we build with and between them.

INTERDEPENDENCE

Throughout this book, I have talked implicitly and explicitly about interdependence. Up until now, I have done so primarily through a technical lens that emphasizes how the parts of an ecosystem exist and interact with both each other and the entire ecosystem. The whole mirrors the parts. Now, I focus on a normative view of interdependence as a belief that supports and enables our classrooms, schools, and districts to behave in ways that fuel and build coherence. In a general sense, interdependence is the belief that people share social and emotional bonds with each other that support their individual and collective well-being and, at the same time, allow everyone to hold a solid sense of themselves within those bonds. We are permeable and permeate the bonds and relationships around us. It is the recognition and acceptance of the repetitive small movements between the people and parts of our ecosystems that are the building blocks of coherence. Each part is independently necessary and valuable. This is true whether our ecosystem is a classroom, school, or district. Clarity and transparency about the roles and functions of each part in supporting the overall purpose of the ecosystem is a priority. Internal accountability is established and reinforced through meaningful communication and feedback about the "purpose and nature of the work" across the system and its parts (Fullan & Quinn, 2016).

When educators believe people share social and emotional bonds with each other that support their individual and collective well-being, we are positioned to cultivate a collective mindset where each member of the system believes in the interdependence of the parts of the system. In our work as educators, interdependence generates a shared desire to "build capacity and ownership among participants" to learn about and adopt the practices and strategies that make coherence in our ecosystems possible (Fullan & Quinn, 2016). As a belief, interdependence also gives us the courage to challenge limiting beliefs like the logic of scarcity, meritocracy, and competition, which cause division, fragmentation, and isolation at every level of our work. Interdependence helps us focus on strengthening the interconnections that exist between the stakeholders in our educational ecosystems and strengthening the interactions that are organized by the systems, structures, and policies in our classrooms, schools, and districts so they support the development of a deeply held collective purpose about our work. Michael Fullan and Jane Quinn, internationally recognized leadership experts, call this coherence and offer this compelling explanation of coherence: "Coherence pertains to people individually and especially collectively. To cut to the chase, coherence consists of the shared depth of understanding about the purpose and the nature of the work. Coherence, then, is what is in the minds of and actions of people individually and collectively" (Fullan & Quinn, 2016). Their definition suggests that coherence is more than "community-building," "alignment," "collaboration," or "integration," which can all be articulated in well-crafted goals and strategies that miss the mark when it comes to implementation. Implementation often fails to launch, derails, or short circuits because the mindset and the culture needed to support the desired changes were not developed throughout the system. "Coherence is an intentionally developed lattice of relationships that connects minds and cultures and prepares them for the work ahead" (Fullan & Quinn, 2016). Coherence is created when we believe in interdependence. Educators cannot move toward emancipatory educational ecosystems without the cultivation of a collective mindset where each member of the system believes in the interdependence of the parts of the system.

EMPOWERMENT

Everyone seeks self-actualization to fully realize the greatest expression of the sparks that exist within us. This drive is as natural as the metamorphosis that occurs when a caterpillar stops eating and spins itself into a tight cocoon where it dissolves its caterpillar tissue and grows the wings, antennae, and legs of the butterfly. Every thought, experience, and moment in our lives contribute to our becoming. Who and what we become emerges from the aggregation of the small pieces of our lives. Because we are human beings and not fish or butterflies, our becoming is not singularly determined by the natural biological processes germane to our species. As I have discussed, our development happens through intimate, on-going interaction with our physical and social environments. We acquire knowledge and develop our beliefs, attitudes, and skills through a dynamic relationship with our external world. Just as the world around us constantly changes, none of us is static in our growth or evolution. We are always becoming.

The purposes of education in this interplay between individuals and society are primarily defined by social and cultural norms and economic needs. Formal education and schooling play a significant role in shaping who we become as citizens and workers, reflecting the existing social hierarchies and inequalities and preparing students to participate in and reproduce them. As I hope I have convincingly shown by now, these realities in the nature and structure of our educational ecosystems are severely limiting to our becoming in general. They are detrimental to the self-actualization of Black students everywhere. If we limit the purposes of education to knowledge acquisition, citizenship, and employment, the peak of Maslow's hierarchy (self-actualization) remains largely inaccessible because such purposes lead us to fulfill social roles that may or may not allow us to pursue or fulfill our unique potential.

Self-actualized people exist all around us. Harriet Tubman, Toni Morrison, and Rhianna are examples of self-actualized Black women who realized the extent of their personal power to take control of their own lives and to use their control creatively in the world. They did this by developing a strong sense of empowerment within themselves. How can we as educators purposefully and intentionally contribute to activating the limitless potential in Black students? We can do this by believing empowerment is a core purpose of education and designing emancipatory educational ecosystems where this belief is activated in ourselves and our students. "Empowerment is a multidimensional social process that helps people gain control over their own lives. It is a process that fosters power (that is, the capacity to implement) in people, for use in their own lives, their communities, and in their society, by acting on issues that they define as important" (Page & Czuba, 1999).

Empowerment unleashes the liberatory power of education that Black educators have historically used to propel the learning of Black children when other resources were denied or scarce (Perry, Steele, & Hilliard, 2003). When empowerment is prioritized, a unifying vision for education that supports student development of autonomy and self-determination is implemented through shared practices at all levels of the ecosystem. Classrooms, schools, and districts are connected to local communities and engage and integrate community resources so that students understand the value of their communities to their learning and also experience how collective power is built. Learning experiences engage students in historical, political, and sociological analysis of their lives, society, and the world. School and district leaders are committed to creating the conditions, developing policies, and providing resources needed across their ecosystem for educators to unapologetically develop content, use instructional strategies, create enrichment opportunities, and use discipline practices "that connect in-school learning to out-of-school living; remote education equity and excellence; create community among individuals from different cultural, social, and ethnic backgrounds; and develop students' agency, efficacy, and empowerment" (Gay, 2018). Empowerment supports educators to believe in and act on our responsibility to do this for our students and ourselves.

"Valuing Where You're From," a lesson developed by the My Brother's Keeper Initiative in Newark, is an example of a learning experience that engages high school students in the historical, political, and sociological analysis of their lives. The lesson demonstrates a change in content, a change in how teachers approach the content, and a change in how students are positioned in their learning. The lesson integrates community mapping with literary analysis to empower students to identify assets in their communities, to draw on each other's perspectives, and expand their understandings of assets through the lens of award-winning Puerto Rican poet and children's book author Willie Perdomo.

VALUING WHERE YOU'RE FROM

Objective

Students will be able to identify the myriad of community assets within their local community by mapping resources that exist and engaging in multiple revisions, considering discussions with their peers, and reading Willie Perdomo's poem "Where I'm From."

Warm-Up

Create a community map.

On a blank page in their notebooks, have students draw a map of their community. They can choose any part of the community (neighborhood around a school) or map a larger region (an entire city). The map can include places, people, streets, landmarks, and any other information students think represents their community.

Once the maps have been generated, place students in groups or pairs to discuss the similarities and differences on their community maps.

Bring the class together for a whole group discussion of their community maps. Chart the similarities and differences of the community maps. Discuss with students why they chose to include the information represented on their community maps. Generate ideas about what their responses suggest is valuable and important in their community.

Learning Activity

After the discussion, have students read "Where I'm From" by Willie Perdomo. As they read the poem, have them compare the things he highlights about his community and how that compares/contrasts with the things they highlighted about their community. Leverage the following guided questions to facilitate the conversation. Students can write responses in a journal and then share aloud.

What elements does Willie Perdomo emphasize about his neighborhood?

There are several descriptive references in this poem. Which references do you see as positive, and which do you see as negative? (This should cause some healthy debate that will help with subsequent lessons regarding cultural wealth.)

Did this poem remind you of something you forgot to highlight about your own community map?

Product/Deliverables

Community map

Journal entries

Assessment Evidence

Community map highlighting the myriad of resources that can be found in their community.

Teaching Tips

Note to teacher: Students should write and keep notes on all activities they engage in as the compilation of these activities will support the GRASP.

Time Frame for Lesson: 50 to 55 minutes

Change cannot be created from the logic of scarcity and deficit-based thinking, which tell us that what we can do and who Black students are is limited. These ideas diminish the confidence of educators and steal opportunities from Black students. Teachers and leaders often struggle to contend with the force deficit beliefs exert daily on their classrooms, schools, and districts. Here are seven shifts that will help integrate these four and other affirming beliefs into the learning in your classroom, school, or district:

1. Infuse affirmation into the language of your educational ecosystem.
2. Move from "do nows" and "anticipatory sets" to community-building activities that use content to build relationships among students, concepts, and their lives beyond school.
3. Integrate local cultural knowledge so that local languages and context are observable in every dimension of the school and classroom culture.
4. Create a student-centered culture that uses students' own knowledge of their lives to build on what they already know while stretching them beyond the familiar.
5. Develop processes and practices that ensure student collaboration and integrate multiple student perspectives, ideas, and outcomes into all aspects of the school and classroom.

6. Use teaching materials (i.e., original documents, documentaries, literature, art and music, testimonials, and interviews) that empower students, raise critical consciousness, and address historical patterns and social dynamics (social relationships, interactions, and issues).
7. Support students to co-create knowledge together and with you, and produce original work.

PAUSE AND PROCESS

Individual Reflection

1. Where in your practice do you see evidence of these affirming beliefs?
2. Where in your practice do these affirming beliefs need attention?
3. Where in your educational ecosystem do you see evidence of these affirming beliefs?
4. Where in your educational ecosystem do these affirming beliefs need attention?
5. Who in your educational ecosystem operates from these affirming beliefs? What can you learn from them?
6. What affirming beliefs would you add?

Collective Planning (in a grade level, department, school, leadership team, parent, community, or other collective meeting space)

Partner with someone in your grade level, content area, school, or at your table. Discuss the presence of affirming beliefs in your educational ecosystem. What commonalities do you find with your partner? Differences? What do you notice about your shared responses? What outlying responses do you observe?

Continue to aggregate the exploration of the presence of affirming beliefs in your educational ecosystem until you culminate with a whole-group discussion about what you collectively notice about the presence of affirming beliefs in your educational ecosystem.

Adopting and habituating ourselves to new beliefs is not a clean or linear process for ourselves or in our educational ecosystems. There are peaks and valleys, triumphs, and failures across the entire path. You bring your whole self to your work as an educator and, therefore, must bring your whole self to the transformation of our beliefs. As I said in Chapter 3, remember, there are as many beliefs, definitions, ideas, and strategies within your educational ecosystem as there are individuals. You will be challenged. Deficit beliefs will surface. Expect it. Recognize and name the challenges and beliefs when they arise. This is the only way to attack deficit beliefs and replace them with affirming beliefs that will inspire and help your ecosystem move toward emancipatory educational ecosystems. When and where there is resistance, amplify how you are practicing conscious collectivism and remind yourself and your educational ecosystem that affirming beliefs are at the heart of collective purpose. Join a national network of teachers or leaders who are further along in their development to support and guide you. Build your knowledge of and capacity for culturally responsive-sustaining education transformation (CRSET). In Chapter 9, I discuss the importance of CRSET to emancipatory educational ecosystems and return to the Hilltop Pilot discussed in Chapter 5 to provide further insights into how stakeholders understand CRSET and its importance to the education of Black students.

Why You Might Resist Beliefs That Affirm Black Students

1. The anti-Blackness and other deficit beliefs present in your thinking and work remain unexamined and unchallenged.
2. The emotions and physical sensations you feel when thinking or speaking beliefs that affirm Black students are uncomfortable or unfamiliar to you.
3. You doubt the significance of beliefs in either your personal and professional life or in the life of your educational system or both.

Additional Resources

Abolitionist Teaching Network. (2020). (rep.). *Guide for racial justice & abolitionist social and emotional learning*.

Watson, D., Hagopian, J., & Au, W. (2018). *Teaching for black lives*. Rethinking Schools.

CHAPTER 9

By Design

Culturally Responsive-Sustaining Educational Transformation (CRSET)

With all the good intentions and stipulations, why is there still not a systemic practice or pedagogy aimed at developing high intellectual performance in all students instead of instilling marginalizing practices for students of color, especially those in urban areas?

—Asa Hilliard

It seems simplistic to think students who feel marginalized, academically abandoned, or invisible in the classroom would reengage simply because we mention tribal kings of Africa or Aztec empires of Mexico in the curriculum or use "call and response" chants to get students pumped up.

—Zaretta Hammond

The most frequent comments I hear about culturally responsive-sustaining education when I teach educational leadership students or lead a professional development session with teachers or school leaders is, "Of course, I think this is important. But it is impossible for me to know everything about every student I have." Teachers typically accompany these statements with questions that ask, "Does this mean I have to create a different lesson plan for every student in my class?" or "Do I have to become an expert on the cultures of all of my students?" School and district leaders raise concerns like, "How do I change the beliefs of my staff so that they understand that 'this' is something we need to address?" or "When do I find the time to add 'this' to our planning?"

These comments reflect an anxiety I generally observe when educators are faced with introducing new programs, curricula, or strategies into their familiar and practiced ways of doing things. However, I have observed that at a larger level, these statements and others like them point to an unspoken, perhaps unconscious, realization that centering culture and race in our systems and work as educators mean changing how we see and do everything.

When I became the director of the Broader Bolder Approach to Education and was partnered with seven school leaders in Newark to design and implement the major school reform initiative that I described in Chapter 2—the Newark Global Village School Zone (NGVZ), I was both excited and daunted by the scale and the scope of this call. The initiative was exciting to me because I saw it as an opportunity to be a part of changing the school experiences of thousands of students and demonstrating what it looks like to design education from an ecological understanding. I was daunted by the scale of the NGVSZ for two reasons. The first and likely obvious reason for the apprehension I felt was that this initiative was massive, involving comprehensive reform of not one but seven individual school ecosystems. But my fear also stemmed from the fact that I had never been a principal and, therefore, felt unprepared and unqualified for the task before me. So I have some personal familiarity with working through overwhelming, ambiguous education change efforts with which I don't have the anticipated or obvious prerequisite knowledge or experience. I overcame these potential barriers first by developing the applied understanding of ecosystems I have shared throughout this book, by building my knowledge.

Learning to see classrooms, schools, and districts as ecosystems helped me see the different parts, components, and functions within and across the seven schools and then help develop that awareness in the school communities I supported. I also learned to examine my beliefs more critically and to listen more actively, specifically in areas where I do not have prior knowledge or experience and even where I do.

Moving to culturally responsive-sustaining education transformation (CRSET) is complex work that involves every domain of education, whether at the classroom, school, or district level. Policies must be changed. Instructional materials and practices replaced. The learning environment reimagined. Roles, responsibilities, and relationship redefined. Resources reallocated. The process is intentional and purposeful. But the force of the "educational survival complex" can make us feel as if we don't know enough, aren't moving fast enough, and aren't strong enough to create affirming and relevant learning experiences for Black students. I have felt all these pressures in all of my work. But as I shared at the end of Chapter 8, it is precisely when these pressures surface that they must be named and the principles for CRSET I share in this chapter must be affirmed in their place. The practice of conscious collectivism—sharing information (data, strategies, experiences, reflections, etc.), learning together, building a common purpose, setting goals and planning, and holding each other accountable for using your collective power, knowledge, and resources—is how CRSET takes roots in your educational ecosystem. The more deeply embedded in conscious collectivism you work to learn about and design CRSET, the more powerful the transformation of your educational ecosystem will be.

CULTURALLY RESPONSIVE-SUSTAINING EDUCATION TRANSFORMATION

My identity as an educator has been shaped by numerous educators, thinkers, and texts that have situated culturally responsive and relevant pedagogy as necessary to transform the learning opportunities and educational experiences of Black students and other historically marginalized groups. My thinking has evolved along with new developments in the theories and practices these approaches offer. These texts, which have professional and personal meaning and significance to me, are what Alfred Tatum calls my "textual lineage" (Tatum, 2009).

You may already be familiar with some of this literature. For example, Ladson-Billings (1994, 2014), who introduced culturally relevant teaching, and Geneva Gay, who introduced culturally responsive pedagogy, are the seminal and foundational threads of my lineage. These foundational frameworks, which I refer to as culturally relevant and responsive pedagogy (CCRP), catalyzed a shift from a deficit lens that focused on what Black students lack to an affirming lens that prioritized "what (is) right about these students" (Ladson-Billings, 2014). Dr. Ladson-Billing's work established teachers' dispositions and attitudes as integral to the instructional choices teachers make. Dr. Gay codified the competencies and methods culturally responsive educators bring to bear in the classroom. Drs. Ladson-Billings's and Gay's frameworks opened the field for thousands of academic articles and resources for educators committed to social justice, cultural competence, and intellectual excellence for Black students (Aronson & Laughter, 2016; Howard, 2017; K. A. Morrison et al., 2008; Muhammad, 2020). Ladson-Billings (2006) pushed us to evolve our thinking beyond the "achievement gap" to the "educational debt" to shift educators' and policy focus onto the laws, policies, and practices that perpetuate inequitable learning opportunities.

My approach to culturally responsive-sustaining education transformation integrates the enduring understandings I have gleaned from Drs. Ladson-Billings and Gay's foundational frameworks with big ideas that have come forward in more recent work: (1) culture, learning, and the brain (Hammond, 2015; Jackson, 2010; Lee, 2008); (2) culturally responsive school leadership (Khalifa et al., 2016); and (3) culturally sustaining pedagogy (Paris & Alim, 2017). It also intersects with the cultural and ecological framework developed by scholar and researcher Carol Lee (2008, 2010, 2017). When braided together, these approaches provide an ecological framework for designing, implementing, and evaluating CRSET that includes ten key principles:

1. Race and racism operate in all educational ecosystems.
2. Culture influences our cognition, perceptions of the world, and how we learn.
3. Leaders establish the systems, policies, culture, and practices that make CRSET possible.
4. Affirming beliefs wire our educational ecosystems to recognize and tap into the genius of students, communities, and educators.
5. Educators need the resources, training, and support that personal and professional transformation requires.
6. Educators' lives outside of classrooms and schools matter to the learning that takes place inside them.
7. Culturally responsive-sustaining competencies and methods empower educators to create powerful learning experiences.
8. Educational experiences that sustain students' cultural, experiential, and linguistic knowledge propel learning.

9. The social, historical, cultural, and political context of classrooms, schools, and districts must be understood and factored into the systems, policies, practices, and content that organize learning.

10. All stakeholders work collectively to share information (data, strategies, experiences, reflections, etc.), learn together, build a common purpose, set goals, design plans, and hold each other accountable for using their collective power, knowledge, and resources to create change.

In Figure 9.1, I outline how these principles work together to shape the learning environment at different levels of an educational ecosystem.

Culturally responsive-sustaining education transformation is the systemic application of these principles to understand, plan, and deliver education at every level of an ecosystem. It is the design of classrooms, schools, and districts where the students' cultural and linguistic experiences, background knowledge, and ways of learning anchor their educational experiences. For students acquiring English as a second or other language, CRSET provides a learning environment that explicitly supports, affirms, and values the home language and culture, honors multilingual learners as a part of a learning community, and encourages them to participate rigorously in new learning opportunities. CRSET also provides entry points for students to sustain and utilize their primary languages as sustenance for their identities. In addition, differentiated learning, the integration of prerequisites, and learning supports afford students with disabilities multi-modal learning opportunities in affirming, safe, and supportive environments. The adoption of CRSET sets in motion the systemic shifts needed to put us on a path to creating emancipatory educational ecosystems where every student is enveloped in a culture where they matter, belong, and are empowered to achieve academically through their culture, identities, and strengths. It prepares us to think about how to create learning environments where, as a student from Hilltops says, students are "Motivated to feel like (themselves) . . . to feel bigger than (how we typically) see (them)." Finally, as Carol Lee suggests, CRSET "takes into consideration teachers' and students' lives outside of school as well as thinking of how classroom life is integrated with school and district organizational practices as well as broader policy implications that include multiple actors" (Lee, 2017).

Ladson-Billings (1994) provides three categories of teaching behaviors: conceptions of self and others, social relations, and knowledge that are actionable at each level of our work. The

FIGURE 9.1

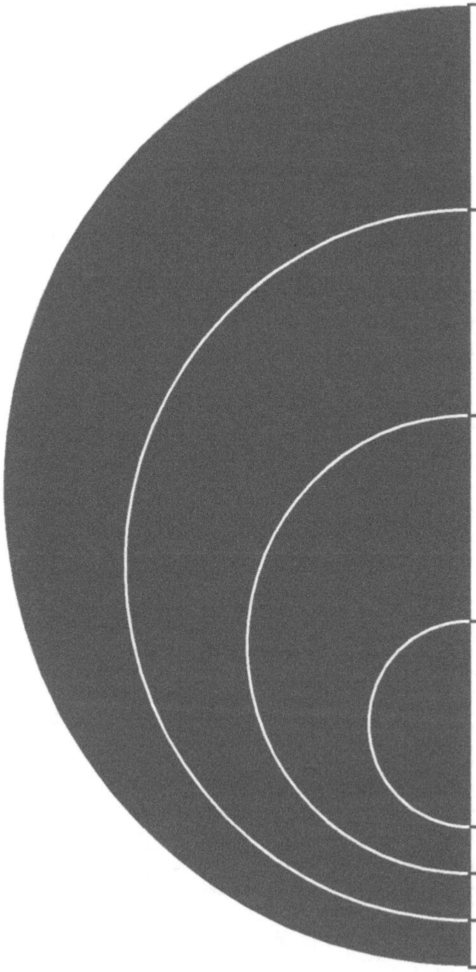

Neighborhood / District Municipality / State / Federal	The social context of the classroom, school, and districts where students learn, for example, state and federal policies, historical context, and common beliefs about and approaches to education. • Builds awareness about and support for learning environments and practices that use students' cultural frames of references and connects to their lived experiences to propel their learning.
Classroom / School/ District	The interactions that occur between the classroom setting, the school environment, and the district, for example, district policies, professional development, or resources for extracurricular opportunities. • Establishes a district culture and structures that support schools to provide learning experiences that use students' cultural frames of reference and connects to their lived experiences to propel their learning.
Classroom / School	The interactions that occur between the classroom and the school environment, and for example, school policies, curricula implementation, or extracurricular opportunities. • Creates a school environment that supports learning experiences that use students' cultural frames of references and connects to their lived experiences to propel their learning.
Classroom	The interactions that occur with the classroom setting. • Provides students with learning experiences that use their cultural frames of reference and connects to their lived experiences to propel their learning.

ten CREST principles I shared previously are aligned with these three categories in Table 9.1.

TABLE 9.1 • The Intersection of Categories of Teaching Behaviors and Principles of Culturally Responsive-Sustaining Educational Transformation

CATEGORIES OF TEACHING BEHAVIORS	TEACHING BEHAVIOR	TEN PRINCIPLES OF CRSET
Conceptions of Self and Others	• Believe that all the students are capable of academic success • See their pedagogy as art—unpredictable, always in the process of becoming • See themselves as members of the community • See teaching as a way to give back to the community • Believe in a Freirean notion of teaching as mining or pulling out	• Culture influences our cognition, perceptions of the world, and how we learn. • Affirming beliefs wire our educational ecosystems to recognize and tap into the genius of students, communities, and educators. • Educators' lives outside of classrooms and schools matter to the learning that takes place inside them.
Social Relations	• Maintain fluid student–teacher relationships • Demonstrate a connectedness with students • Develop a community of learners • Encourage students to learn collaboratively and be responsible for one another	• Race and racism operate in all educational ecosystems. • Leaders establish the systems, policies, culture, and practices that make CRSET possible. • Educators need the resources, training, and support that personal and professional transformation requires. • All stakeholders work collectively to share information (data, strategies, experiences, reflections, etc.), learn together, build a common purpose, set goals, design plans, and hold each other accountable for using their collective power, knowledge, and resources.
Knowledge	• Knowledge is not static • Knowledge must be viewed critically • Teachers must be passionate about knowledge and learning • Teachers must scaffold, or build bridges, to facilitate learning • Assessment must be multifaceted, incorporating multiple forms of excellence	• Educational experiences that sustain students' cultural, experiential, and linguistic knowledge propel learning. • Culturally responsive-sustaining competencies and methods empower educators to create powerful learning experiences. • The social, historical, cultural, and political context of classrooms, schools, and districts must be understood and factored into the systems, policies, and practices that organize learning.

Whether you are a classroom teacher, a counselor or social worker, a school administrator, a district supervisor, or a superintendent, you can apply these domains and principles to your work in your educational ecosystem. In Table 9.2, I provide examples of questions that we can ask ourselves to help us think about how to apply the seven CREST principles in each domain from our different roles.

TABLE 9.2 ● Inquiry for the Application of the Principles of Culturally Responsive-Sustaining Educational Transformation

CATEGORY	TEACHER	SUPPORT STAFF	SCHOOL ADMINISTRATOR	DISTRICT SUPERVISOR	SUPERINTENDENT
Conceptions of Self and Others	How do I show each of my students I believe in their genius and the genius of their community? How do I nurture this belief in my classroom?	How do I show each of my students I believe in their genius and the genius of their community? How do I nurture this belief in my school?	How do I support my school staff to develop the belief in the genius of each student and the genius of their community? How do I nurture this belief in my school?	How do I support each of my department chairs, coaches, etc., to support teachers to develop the belief in the genius of students and communities? How do I nurture this belief in their departments?	How do I support each of my principals to support teachers to develop the belief in the genius of their students and communities? How do I nurture this belief in my district?
Social Relations	What strategies do I use to build relationships with my students and to help them build relationships with other students?	What strategies do I use to build relationships with my students and to help them build relationships with other students?	What strategies do I use to build relationships with my school staff and to help them build relationships with their students and each other?	What strategies do I use to build relationships with the staff I support and to help them build relationships across content areas and with each other?	What strategies do I use to build relationships with principals and to help them build relationships across schools and with each other?
Conceptions of Knowledge	What opportunities do I provide students to use their cultural frames of reference and lived experience to understand, build on, and challenge the knowledge in their learning?	What opportunities do I provide students to use their cultural frames of reference and lived experience to support their learning and personal development?	What opportunities do I provide for my school staff to use their professional experience to guide their professional development and build their capacity to provide opportunities for students to use their cultural frames of reference and lived experience in the learning?	What opportunities do I provide for the staff I support to use their professional experience to guide their professional development and build their capacity to provide opportunities for students to use their cultural frames of reference and lived experience in their learning?	What opportunities do I provide for principals to use their professional experience to guide their professional development and build their capacity to provide opportunities for students to use their cultural frames of reference and lived experience in their learning?

PAUSE AND PROCESS

Individual Reflection

Rate your awareness of the ten CRSET principles from 1 (least awareness) to 10 (most awareness). You may give more than one principle the same rating.

After rating your individual awareness, rate how much each of the ten CRSET principles is observable in your educational ecosystem (consider systems, policies, and practices) from 1 (least observable) to 10 (most observable). You may give more than one principle the same rating.

1. Race and racism operate in all educational ecosystems.
2. Culture influences our cognition, perceptions of the world, and how we learn.
3. Leaders establish the systems, policies, culture, and practices that make CRSET possible.
4. Affirming beliefs wire our educational ecosystems to recognize and tap into the genius of students, communities, and educators.
5. Educators need the resources, training, and support that personal and professional transformation requires.
6. Educators' lives outside of classrooms and schools matter to the learning that takes place inside them.
7. Culturally responsive-sustaining competencies and methods empower educators to create powerful learning experiences.
8. Educational experiences that sustain students' cultural, experiential, and linguistic knowledge propel learning.
9. The social, historical, cultural, and political context of classrooms, schools, and districts must be understood and factored into the systems, policies, practices, and content that organize learning.
10. All stakeholders work collectively to share information (data, strategies, experiences, reflections, etc.), learn together, build a common purpose, set goals, design plans, and hold each other accountable for using their collective power, knowledge, and resources to create change.

(Continued)

(Continued)

Collective Planning (in a grade level, department, school, leadership team, parent, community, or other collective meeting space)

Partner with someone in your grade level, content area, school, or at your table. Discuss your ratings. What commonalities do you find with your partner? Differences? What outliers are there? What questions are raised for you?

Continue to aggregate the rankings until you culminate with a whole-group discussion about what your collective ratings suggest about the needs of your educational ecosystem as they relate to CRSET.

NO MORE DREAMS DEFERRED: CRSET MATTERS AND EVERYONE HAS A ROLE TO PLAY

In Chapter 4, I shared insights about how students and teachers feel when they are in classrooms and schools from a CRSE pilot I conducted in the Hilltop School District in 2017. The remainder of this chapter draws on the voices of stakeholders from the Hilltop pilot to provide a deeper look at how this district approached developing an understanding about CRSET across the district and the strategies stakeholders identified as important to the adoption of a CRSET framework.

In addition to the students and teachers I interviewed as a part of the Hilltop pilot study, central office administrators, school board members, and principals from the district were also interviewed. Additionally, over 9,000 parents responded to the survey question, "How important is it for your child's education to be connected to their culture, community, and interests?" included on a parent information form. Ninety-two percent of the parents who answered the survey question responded that it was very important or moderately important for their child's education to be connected to their culture, community, and interests. Eighteen percent of the responding parents also provided an explanation about their response. Cumulatively, these data provide unprecedented insight into a district's views about CSRET.

From these data, four major themes about why CRSET is important to the education of the students in Hilltop Schools emerged: (1) the diversity of the city, (2) students' engagement in their learning, (3) developing positive identities, and (4) students understanding where they come from. Quotes from a cross-section of stakeholders capture the essence of these themes (see Table 9.3):

TABLE 9.3 ● How Hilltop Stakeholders Think About Culturally Responsive Education

QUESTION	IS CULTURALLY RESPONSIVE EDUCATION IMPORTANT TO EDUCATING STUDENTS?
Parent	My child needs to understand where he comes from and how other cultures are different. How our community is. How people are with each other.
Principal	Yes, it is. If you look at the demographics of our community, we are not a monolithic society. There is not one strategy that is going to work for the demographics of our city. We marginalize many students when we continue to do this traditional, one way of education.
Central Office Administrator	Yes, Because we have to start thinking about kids on another level to keep them engaged. I see a high level of disengagement among students.
Community Member	Yes, because when children learn about the significance of who they are, it builds self-esteem. And in building self-esteem in students, you can begin to open their minds. Their minds are like sponges. If they can believe in themselves, they can achieve the curriculum.
School Board Member	A child should know where they are from. The Puerto Rican generation today is very different from the generation that came in the '40s and the '50s. The problem is this younger generation doesn't understand what it means to be Puerto Rican. The heritage. Family that worked in sugar cane fields. To me, it is very important that children know where they are from. If you don't, you get lost.

The full scope of the Hilltop pilot study is beyond this book. What is important is that participants recognized that CRSET is a paradigm shift that will not happen when disconnects exist between schools and communities, teachers and students, or parents and teachers. CRSET was understood by the stakeholders interviewed as a collective endeavor that involves and creates community. Building relationships with students and their families, as well as with the surrounding community, was at the core of how stakeholders talked about what CRSET meant to them. The following quotes are examples of the ways in which stakeholders centered relationships and connections in their views of CRSET (see Table 9.4).

TABLE 9.4 • What Culturally Responsive Education Means to Hilltop Stakeholders

QUESTION	WHAT DOES CULTURALLY RESPONSIVE EDUCATION MEAN TO US?
Teacher	Being culturally responsive is tailoring your lessons to appeal to students' interests and cultures. However, you need to be conscious of the slippery slope that not all students are alike. You need to build relationships with every individual student, because every student may have different interests. So, you can differentiate your lesson for each child based on each child.
Community Member	The tone in the district needs to be some different kind of way to approach the parents. They have one or two back-to-school nights. To help parents through the process of education is to open the doors. Utilize the support parents need.
Student	An education process that involves everyone pertaining to the individual. Microcosm and macrocosm where the global affects the individual and vice versa. My teacher, my family, and friends are all involved in the educational process I am going through. This global development of the individual. Doing all of that and incorporating different cultures.
Teacher	To have a community of teachers, scholars, and parents. I feel like culture needs to be strengthened because we are missing the parent part. That will help us understand the whole kid. That is what culturally responsive is, understanding the whole culture of the kids' socioeconomics, background, norms—everything affects them. So, we can better service them. Gender identity as well.

The centrality of social relations to classroom instruction, how schools and the district engage parents, integrating the diversity of cultures in classrooms and schools, and educating the whole child stands out in these stakeholders' conceptions of CRSET. These stakeholders' views about what CRSET is suggested that a culturally responsive-sustaining learning environment actively engages its ecosystem as a learning community to identify and generate the learning experiences that meet student needs and "appeal to students' interest and culture." Though we often think about CRSET as it relates to race, ethnicity, and culture, as the quotes that follow highlight, the specific needs of students as they relate to gender identity, sexual orientation, language, and special education were also identified in this pilot as a characteristic participants associated with CRSET (see Table 9.5).

TABLE 9.5 ● What Intersectionality and Culturally Responsive-Sustaining Education Means to Hilltop Stakeholders

QUESTION	WHAT DOES CULTURALLY RESPONSIVE EDUCATION MEAN TO US?
Principal	The district has sent us to workshops about LGBT student needs. I have seen a couple of different workshops provided.
Principal	They are shifting. SPED is emphasizing inclusion, which is the district's mindset to have inclusive processes for students and classrooms.
Teacher	Being aware of their linguistic needs. What they need to succeed in the new environment, new home, and culture.

Cumulatively, these views suggest that each actor in students' educational ecosystems, including students themselves, contributes important information to the learning, development, and social-emotional needs of students.

CULTURALLY RESPONSIVE-SUSTAINING EDUCATION AND SYSTEMS CHANGE: IT'S NOT JUST FOR TEACHERS AND CLASSROOMS

The Hilltop Schools pilot provides many insights about how the stakeholders across an ecosystem might think it necessary to approach CRSET in their schools and districts. This section shares these insights and demonstrates the significance of a systemic framework to guide how a school or district approaches CRSET. Leadership, vision and planning, knowledge building, resources, and collaboration were the primary strategies that emerged from this pilot study. In each of the following sections, I share the lessons about each strategy from the pilot study. In sharing these lessons, I speak directly to you, my reader, as both an acknowledgment that, in some way, you have the opportunity and responsibility to influence your ecosystem and from the hope that you will take these lessons and use them to do so.

LEADERSHIP

The implementation of CRSET rests on your leadership at every level of the system. You have the will to unapologetically establish CRSET as the standard for education in your ecosystems. You drive the learning, dialogue, planning, and implementation of CRSET in departments, schools, and classrooms. As a leader, you also allocate resources in ways that reflect the priorities of CRSET and create roles that have responsibility for focusing, supporting, and monitoring the work. You bring your ecosystem together to create the systems, policies, structures, and practices that will allow CRSET to become the foundation of the learning experiences of students in their classrooms and schools.

Leadership Practice Example: After months of school and community meetings, Jones High School has been approved by the district to have the autonomy to implement CRSET; the principal, Mr. Gardner, brings the entire school community to the auditorium to announce the news. Mr. Gardner tells the students, staff, parents, and community members gathered that "We will be able to do the things we've been talking about doing. We will be able to add ethnic studies, new ELA, history, and other courses. But we have a lot of work to do together, learning and planning how to become the school we want to be. So I need you to tell other parents to attend the meetings. I need you to tell your children to get involved. I need you to bring your classmates. Staff, I need you to hold each other, to hold me accountable for putting the things in place that we need to make these changes. It's time to be empowered. I need you all to be the magnificent people you are intended to be."

KNOWLEDGE BUILDING: RESEARCH, PROFESSIONAL DEVELOPMENT, TRAINING, AND EXAMPLES

Learning about CRSE, knowing what it looks like in practice, and understanding how to plan for and implement it is core to making CRSET the learning framework for your educational ecosystem. You provide professional development and training to everyone in your ecosystem, from members of the school board and community to security guards and aids in schools and, of course, your students and teachers. You engage teachers and other staff to develop a continuous learning plan that provides job-embedded professional development (the focus of common planning time team meetings and leadership team meetings) and includes learning opportunities for parents and other nonschool personnel in the education ecosystem. You recognize the need for extensive learning from professionals in the field about CRSET and identify learning from examples of CRSET in classrooms, schools, and districts that are like yours as important learning opportunities for helping your educational ecosystem understand what CRSET is in practice.

Knowledge Building Practice Example: Mrs. Hamilton is a fourth-grade teacher. At a recent conference, she saw Dr. Yvette Jackson give a presentation on the Pedagogy of Confidence and rushed out to buy the book *Pedagogy of Confidence: Inspiring High Intellectual Performance in Urban Schools*. Mrs. Hamilton shares the book with her principal, who also reads it and talks to Mrs. Hamilton about leading a team of teachers to plan how they can use the book to launch the entire school into a learning series. Mrs. Hamilton and a group of teachers develop the plan and contact Dr. Jackson for her input and to ask her to come to the school to provide job-embedded professional development to help them understand and use the book in their instructional planning for the coming year and a series of community learning opportunities for parents, community members, and other non-school personnel in the school.

VISION AND PLANNING

You bring your ecosystem together to collaboratively develop a shared vision and a shared plan for CRSET. You understand that while you are responsible for initiating the processes for developing a shared vision and plan for CRSET, the development is inclusive, collaborative, and generative. You view shared vision and planning as important to communicating a coherent and unifying message about your ecosystem's collectively held priorities and to designing the framework your ecosystem needs to embed CRSET in your systems, structures, policies, and practices.

Vision and Planning Practice Example: Ms. Ervin is a first-year principal. Her school district is midway through developing a new strategic plan. She decides that while the district plan is being finalized, it would be a good time for her school to begin creating its own plan. Ms. Ervin begins meeting with her leadership to develop a strategic planning process that will include all of the school's staff, engage students, and integrate parent and community voices. The leadership team suggests that teachers, students, and parents should also be added to the strategic planning team so that their ideas and voices about how to conduct the process are heard from the beginning and not once an outline of the process has been created or only as a part of community meetings. Ms. Ervin partners the school with a local university to engage experts in CRSET to guide them through how to make their planning process culturally responsive and sustaining, provide professional development and community learning experiences about CRSET, and support the design of their school plan.

RESOURCES

You understand that resources and how you allocate them are a signal that CRSET is valued in your ecosystem. You recognize the systemic and structural inequities that create barriers to learning for your students and dedicate resources to addressing them. You explicitly redirect and allocate resources to plan for, design, and implement CRSET. You welcome community resources and opportunities as valuable contributions to CRSET. You engage your ecosystem in collaborative decision-making about resources and their use in your ecosystem. You advocate for the resources your ecosystem needs to implement CRSET.

Resources Practice Example: Jones High School is a neighborhood high school that received most of its students from four elementary schools. Many students move between elementary schools before ultimately attending Jones. Jones is awarded a major grant from a foundation to redesign the content and instruction of the school based on CRSET. As a part of the grant application, Jones allocates a portion of the professional development funds to providing CRSET professional development to the teachers and support staff of the four other schools in the neighborhood and a portion toward offering the cultural enrichment programs and opportunities at the high school to the middle-school students at each of the schools.

COLLABORATION

You understand that relationships and collaboration are central to CRSET. You see collaboration as a distinct component of CRSET that creates purposeful policies and practices for the engagement of your ecosystem. You establish systems, policies, routines, and practices that bring stakeholders to talk to and learn from each other and ensure the integration of students, family, and community voices in decision-making processes. You provide time, structures, and resources for sustained learning partnerships to be established at all levels of the educational ecosystem.

Collaboration Practice Example: The English department at Carter Middle School has been working with faculty in the Center for Pedagogy at the local university for three years to redesign the ELA curricula so that it centers the history, culture, contributions, and voices of students and their communities. There is substantial evidence that the content and instructional changes they have made have increased the engagement and learning of their students. The principal asks if the teachers can support their colleagues in other content areas to learn and implement the planning processes they have adopted. The principal works with the Center for Pedagogy to identify funding for curriculum development. The ELA teachers work together with the Center for Pedagogy to develop a plan for supporting their colleagues and begin providing job-embedded professional development, coaching, and planning to other teams of teachers across content areas.

PAUSE AND PROCESS

Individual Reflection

1. After reading this book, what expectations do you hold as non-negotiable for designing emancipatory educational ecosystems?
2. How will you/do you advocate for these expectations?

Collective Planning (in a grade level, department, school, leadership team, parent, community, or other collective meeting space)

Partner with someone in your grade level, content area, school, or at your table. Discuss the expectations you hold as non-negotiable for designing emancipatory educational ecosystems. What commonalities do you find with your partner? Differences? What do you notice about the expectation you identify? What outlying expectations do you observe?

Continue to aggregate the exploration of the expectations you hold as non-negotiable for designing emancipatory educational ecosystems until you culminate with a whole-group discussion about what you collectively notice about the expectations you hold and how you will advocate for them in your educational ecosystem.

Why You Might Resist Culturally Responsive-Sustaining Education Transformation

1. You fear getting "it" wrong.
2. You have not examined how your cultural frame of reference impacts your practice or considered how you participate in the marginalization of Black students.
3. You are waiting for test scores to prove that Black students deserve to see themselves in their learning.

Additional Resources

Culturally Responsive School Leadership Institute. (n.d.). Retrieved January 22, 2023, from https://www.crsli.org/

Lee, C. D. (2017). An ecological framework for enacting culturally sustaining pedagogy. In D. Paris & H. S. Alim (Eds.), *Culturally sustaining pedagogies: Teaching and learning for justice in a changing world* (pp. 261–273). Teachers College Press.

Epilogue

Emancipate yourselves from mental slavery

None but ourselves can free our minds.

—Bob Marley

How many times have you heard or sung along to Bob Marley's "Redemption Song"? The final song on the last album Marley would release with the Wailers before cancer took his life in 1981, "Redemption Song," is a political song on an album titled *Uprising*. In "Redemption Song," Marley pays homage to Jamaican Pan-Africanist leader Marcus Garvey, who founded the Universal Negro Improvement Association (UNIA) and mobilized an international movement for Black political economic independence. The words "emancipate yourself from mental slavery, none but ourselves can free our minds" come from the speech *The Hand That Works*, delivered by Garvey in 1937, who said, "We are going to emancipate ourselves from mental slavery because whilst others might free the body, none but ourselves can free the mind. Mind is your only ruler, sovereign" (Garvey, 1938). Marley also sings in metaphors about the transatlantic slave trade, systemic oppression, spiritual power, and mental freedom. A decolonized mind, cultural identity, and commitment to justice are, for both men, the essence of emancipation from mental slavery. Both men speak directly to Black people, pressing us to claim our own power to cleanse our minds of the beliefs and ideologies that oppress Black people. Marley's iconic stature and global appeal gave him a platform that still reaches all racial and ethnic groups, allowing him to impress upon his non-Black listeners that they are responsible for eradicating the same beliefs and ideologies within their minds. As Hernández (2022) points out, "the ongoing silent acceptance of anti-Blackness implicates many other racial and ethnic groups in the United States as well as across the globe."

In this book, we have explored how white supremacy, anti-Blackness, and other deficit beliefs create toxic learning environments and inhibit educators from conceiving and creating learning where Black students experience the expansiveness of their minds, the significance of their culture, and the possibilities of their genius. Emancipatory educational ecosystems are classrooms, schools, districts, and communities that purposefully and intentionally work to uproot these beliefs and nurture affirming beliefs and CRSET in their place. But you cannot make this shift without first excavating the beliefs you bring with you to your work and understanding how what you do individually and collectively is influenced by them (Sealey-Ruiz, n.d.). This book asks you to examine what you say you believe and what you do, jump into the gap in between, and feel compelled to take a hard, honest look at what you find so you can do something about it. Educators deeply want to feel good about their work. Educators also want to feel safe. As a result, many avoid naming, calling out, and owning the savage realities that Black students encounter in their learning, particularly when found where you are.

As I was listening to "Redemption Song" one day while writing this book, the lines "How long shall they kill our prophets, while we stand aside and look," in which Marley alludes to the assassinations of Dr. King, Malcolm X, and other powerful Black social leaders, took on new meaning to me. These lines became a metaphor for the "spirit murder" Love (2019) calls out as the malignant impact the "educational survival complex" has on Black students. The anguish in the words of this student expresses the gravity of the negation, pain, and loss Black students feel when their spirits are being murdered in classrooms and schools that should be giving them life.

> It's sad, tiring, draining, and depressed. There's no spark. There's no pull to be in this school. The teachers don't show me why it's great to be Black. My mom raised me to be proud of where I came from, and in school, I feel like that's being suppressed. I'm not being taught about myself or where I come from. And if we are talking about Black people, it's not about the good or a celebration of the greatness that Black people bring to the world. . . . When I walk in the door of the school, it makes me not want to do my work the way I used to. The joy I had at home automatically leaves my body when I step foot into the school.

If you are unwilling to mine the depths of your consciousness and deconstruct the architecture of your educational ecosystem to identify how white supremacy and anti-Blackness operate in both, you are complicit in the spirit murder of Black students. Black students need you to emancipate yourselves and your classrooms, schools, and districts from white supremacy and anti-Blackness so you can build the knowledge and capacity you need to facilitate learning experiences that encounter every Black child as a prophet waiting to bloom. Your students deserve nothing less.

Afterword

By Ras Baraka

This book takes a powerful and instructive look at why it is necessary to address racism and white supremacy in our educational institutions and the serious negative outcomes that come as a result of not addressing them. But more importantly, it seeks to guide us on how we actually can do that effectively and begin to include millions of Americans who have been deliberately excluded from America's educational institutions. The effects of this exclusion are real and long standing. Our efforts to address school improvement through rigor and academic growth in the interest of equity will have limited effect until we acknowledge and remedy the systemic barriers to inclusion.

In 1954, the *Brown v. Board of Education* Supreme Court case challenged segregation in schools and pointed out the moral and undemocratic inconsistencies that were the foundation of Jim Crow and segregation. Prior research substantiated the legal argument put forth in *Brown*. Most notably, Dr. Kenneth and Mamie Clark used what is now known as the "Doll Study" to point out that segregation or white supremacy was not just morally and constitutionally wrong but also had a negative, even debilitating effect on the psyches of Black children. The subjects of this research—253 Black children, ages 3 to 7—when presented with a choice between dolls that looked like them or white-skinned dolls with blonde hair, assigned positive attributes to the white dolls and negative attributes ("bad," "ugly") to the dark-skinned, black-hair dolls. The Clarks, who later served as expert witnesses in the *Brown* case, had a lasting influence on the civil rights movement. Much in the way that the Clarks underscored the harmful effects of racism on young children, I believe this book seeks to do something similar by pointing out the harm caused by destructive educational institutions with regards to race and culture. At the same time, it offers a remedy to such harm by describing how and why equitable, culturally relevant and sustaining educational institutions and curricula can in fact begin to abate the negative outcomes of institutionalized racism and challenge our students to perform at high levels.

I am the mayor of the City of Newark, New Jersey's largest city. My city is predominantly Black and brown, where the average income is around 34,000 dollars, a stark contrast to other cities in the same county whose average income is well over 100,000 dollars. We are also positioned in a state that has one of the largest wealth gaps in the nation between white families and Black and brown families. The state's school system is also one of the top six most segregated districts in the nation. In Newark, more than 90 percent of the students attend schools that are segregated by both race and class because of deliberate systems that have been in place and were never dismantled, even 70 years after *Brown v. Board of Education.*

For more than twenty years, I was also an educator in Newark Public Schools. I started off as a substitute teacher, went through the ranks, and ended my career there as the principal of Central High School. So my view of schools and systems is not only informed by my role as the mayor of the city but even more clearly from the point of view of someone who navigated this system every day, trying to find opportunities to allow my students countless ways to see themselves in the school buildings where they found themselves and, more importantly, to see themselves as beautiful, as necessary, and reflected in stories where they win. This was more important than anything else we did, particularly when their lived experiences have told them the opposite in almost every institution they encountered—especially schools. This foundation was essential to their growth. It is the cornerstone that all other academic and life achievements rest on.

So as Dr. Wells describes clearly, our intent has to be identified and serve to dismantle these imbedded systems that exclude Black and brown children, not just academically but emotionally. She also points out how these institutions go even farther than just making us invisible but to cause deliberate harm in instances through teaching methodology and curriculum that undermine Black and brown children's self-esteem and their ability to self-actualize.

I recently led a roundtable discussion with high school principals and teachers aimed at plotting a pathway out of the debilitating harm of Covid-19 on our students. A former student addressed us at the beginning of the discussion. He had graduated from Newark Public Schools, attended the New Jersey Institute of Technology (NJIT), and was now working at a firm leading the development of new green technologies. What stood out most to me about his story was his emphasis on how much "confidence" played an integral role in his ability to get a scholarship to NJIT and ultimately finish his college career. He was a typical student from Newark. He was an athlete in a comprehensive high school in our city and was offered a college program that he had to complete while in school that competed with his football aspirations. The program was difficult, and he was mired in peer pressure. He explained that the teachers, the environment in his high school, and his professors at the university program gave him the confidence he needed by creating the space that challenged him, allowed him to fail and start again, and made him believe that he actually belonged in the spaces he was placed in and that he would eventually win. He went on to make the point that Dr. Wells is arguing in this book: that he was no different from many of the other students who were not in the program—their beginnings were the same as his. He pointed out that they too could pass that class, navigate that program, and also graduate from NJIT, as he had done. They just needed the confidence. And how do you create confidence, self-worth, belonging, even aptitude when the institutions that you are in have been explicitly designed to or implicitly create the opposite result?

There Are No Deficits Here is even more essential now because our children are especially unsafe as their history and culture have become center stage to the talking points of white supremacists masquerading as public servants. More than 1,000 books have been banned nationwide along with the passage of policies and laws created to further isolate our children and undermine their self-esteem. How can we educate our children in an environment that has been a very contradiction to their growth, in a system designed to ensure that they do not succeed, with books that purposefully exclude them and curricula that erases them, in schools structured to exacerbate their burdens rather than to lift them, and in classrooms that ignore their trauma? Too often, they are forced to sit in front of people who don't even like them, or they are led by people who believe in their inferiority and whose most creative act is forcing them to spend more time and more remediation, where the expectation is that educators prepare them to pass tests that do not measure intellect, capacity, or thinking while they endure disempowering learning that undermines their courage to call out the barriers that prevent them from being successful or building the collective strength to move themselves. We can't ignore inequity and try to get our children to succeed in spite of it. It is on *us* to call out inequity and get them to succeed so they can help us eliminate it. *They* already know that what they are getting is not what everyone else is getting. They know their curriculum was not written for them. The pipelines to which others have access are few and far between for them. They know that just a few miles away in the same county they inhabit, the world is noticeably separate and unequal.

Dr. Wells calls on us to imagine a place without shackles and limitations, a place where our children don't need to struggle just to make it or be equal with the children who started this race long before the whistle was blown. Educating our children must begin with creating conditions in which their value is mirrored back to them. This is the only real defense they have and the only thing that will make the world of school relevant to them. If we are not arming our children with self-worth, then we are handicapping them and praying that some of them, like our New Jersey Tech graduate, break free, against all odds, from so many under our care. We try to make them learn despite the barriers instead of removing them. As a result, we come up with inflexible policies and harsh rules that make them believe they can no longer be children—or worse, mistakes or errors are not human. To err is the learn. Ironically as adults, we know the pathway to success is littered with failure every step of the way. Beating people in a high-stakes competition never leads to victory: Only feeding their imagination will do that. And if they can't imagine themselves in the places we have created for them, it doesn't matter how much we confine them: They will always find a way to escape, even if it's emotionally.

I completely understand what Dr. Wells envisions because I was blessed to be a part of the process called the *Global Village School Zone* from the *Broader and Bolder Approach* (BBA) created by Dr. Pedro Noguera and enacted by Dr. Lauren Wells. The BBA came to Newark's Central Ward and helped us identify and implement educational policies and practices that actively engaged and built community along with our feeder schools. We began to outline what our immediate community was, and we began to identify the components of our ecosystem. We included every school that fed into the high school where I was the principal. We also engaged places of worship, community-based organizations, block groups, and the local precinct. We began to meet as principals across the zone to plan vertically, to create cross school interactions and programming. We opened our schools as places for community meetings to take place. The community sports teams used our fields, our gym, our pool. We held job fairs and community events. We began to redesign curriculum and paid teachers to continue in that effort over the summer. We created more culturally relevant and community-inspired course work. We created extended day programming using community-based groups and social service agencies. We addressed the social and emotional problems of our children. A health clinic was placed within my school. We plastered our school with quotes from relevant writers and thinkers who looked like our students. We put pictures all over the building of people they could recognize and aspire to be. We let them see themselves as beautiful on purpose. We allowed their parents in the building and organized them to help us not with just behavioral issues but also to do walkthroughs in classrooms to help improve instruction. As a result of all of that, we witnessed double-digit growth, and our graduation rates began to soar. This experience validated what I felt for a very long time: We had to have a very serious deep engagement with the community we were in, and it's impossible to have a deep engagement if you can't see that community or, worse, allow students to see themselves in everything you do from the books you read and the lessons you create to the daily rituals you have put in place.

There is no way that we can separate our children from the inequity they face in the world or the contradictions they come across. Our job is to equip them to solve these issues, to provoke their imagination and creativity, to change what they experience, and enhance all that is good. And we can do this by creating a universal entry point for all of us, not despite our differences but because of them. In fact, the answer to all of this resides in our differences and lived experiences of race, gender, religion, culture. We must teach with this in mind very deliberately because no one wants to build a future that they can't see themselves in.

Appendix

TOOL 1: CONSCIOUS COLLECTIVISM ACTION TOOL

Shifting to conscious collectivism requires a personal commitment to challenge and change how we work with our students, parents, communities, and other stakeholders to design emancipatory educational ecosystems. The Conscious Collectivism Action Tool helps us think about how we can each individually push our systems to develop the policies, practices, and strategies that will foster conscious collectivism in classrooms, schools, or districts. This tool can also be used at the macro levels of an ecosystem (municipality or state). While completing this exercise, you identify your readiness to embrace conscious collectivism (individual), how you can contribute to conscious collectivism in your ecosystem (structural), and the actionable strategies you can take to make conscious collectivism part of your practice (strategies) (Pollock et al., 2010).

Individual: How can you apply the components of conscious collectivism in your role?

Structural: What acts can you take in your role that can counteract large patterns of racial inequality in how students, parents, and other stakeholders are engaged?

Strategies: What methods, techniques, procedures, or processes can you employ in your role to make conscious collectivism part of your practice?

	WHAT CAN I DO? INDIVIDUAL	WHAT CAN I DO? STRUCTURAL	WHAT CAN I DO? STRATEGIES
Collective Context			
Collective Planning			
Collective Purpose			

CONSCIOUS COLLECTIVISM ACTION TOOL: TEACHER EXAMPLE

	WHAT CAN I DO? INDIVIDUAL	WHAT CAN I DO? STRUCTURAL	WHAT CAN I DO? STRATEGIES
Collective Context	Inquire about the thoughts, feelings, experiences, and beliefs of my students, their parents, and colleagues. Know my history and the history of those around me.	Advocate and hold the school accountable for including the least heard voices in our planning, etc. Recognize that different types of information are important to our work. It's not just student achievement data that matters.	Ask "why?" and "why not?" consistently. Begin each school year by creating a classroom education history wall so the class can learn from each other's past experiences.
Collective Planning	Identify how the content areas can be applied in different areas of my work. Engage my students, parents, and colleagues in a root-cause analysis of a challenge in my classroom.	Identify and challenge classroom, school, and district policies and practices that create barriers to conscious collectivism. Monitor my behavior and privilege when participating in mixed-group work, and don't be afraid to hold others accountable for doing the same.	Identify existing opportunities that can become more open, public, or transparent. Embed participatory planning in my students' curricula, so their ideas become integrated into the classroom learning and they learn how to direct their education.
Collective Purpose	Be able to articulate my goals and expectations of education and the larger community. Actively listen to my students' and their parents' goals and expectations of education and for the goals and expectations of the larger community.	Attend conferences and workshops that give me an understanding of how my beliefs and experiences impact my classroom and school. Identify opportunities for collective learning and reflection to be embedded in the school/district.	Over-communicate the shared beliefs of the class in different ways as needed. Give parents the opportunity to observe and provide feedback on the class.

EDUCATIONAL ECOSYSTEMS

TOOL 2: IDENTIFYING ECOSYSTEMS

REFLECTION QUESTION	ECOSYSTEM #1 ________	ECOSYSTEM #2 ________
What are two examples of ecosystems that resonate with you?		
What captures your attention about these ecosystems?		
What components of these ecosystems can you identify?		
How do the ecosystems you identify operate?		

TOOL 3: DEFINING YOUR EDUCATIONAL ECOSYSTEM

REFLECTION QUESTION	ECOSYSTEM #1 ________
What are the components of your educational ecosystem?	
Where do you fit in this ecosystem?	
What operating principles and/or beliefs can you identify that govern how your ecosystem operates?	
How do these operating principles affect Black students in your ecosystem?	

TOOL 4: IDENTIFYING HOW RACE WORKS IN OUR EDUCATIONAL ECOSYSTEMS

Examine the five levels of Bronfenbrenner's Ecosystems Theory in the table that follows and think about how racial beliefs and ideologies influence patterns of social interaction in each example. What other examples of interaction come to mind for you? In the last column, identify how racial beliefs and ideologies impact these interactions.

SYSTEM LEVEL	DEFINITION	EXAMPLES	THE INFLUENCE OF RACIAL BELIEFS AND IDEOLOGIES
Microsystem	A *microsystem* comprises activities and relationships experienced in a face-to-face setting. They also contain other people and often imply systems of belief.	A child's family, nursery or playgroup, neighbors, and their community. The relationship between a child and a principal, teacher, or school counselor.	Assumptions are made about who a child plays with, what they do outside of school, or what their homelife is like.
Mesosystem	The *mesosystem* is all about the links and processes that occur between multiple settings. It is a collection (or system) of microsystems.	Teacher conference with a parent or guardian at the school. A school provides before and after care to accommodate parents' work schedules.	
Exosystem	The *exosystem* includes the links and processes between two or more settings. Sometimes the setting does not include the developing person but still has an influence on that person and their immediate setting.	A parent deployed by the military. The relationship between the home and the guardian's workplace. The relationship between the school and the neighborhood group.	
Macrosystem	The *macrosystem* is the social context in which a child lives and grows up and may be thought of as a societal blueprint that includes the beliefs, systems, laws, social structures, and narratives that organize a society.	The impact of Covid-19 on the child's housing arrangements. School closures due to budget cuts or reform strategies.	Policies are developed that target behaviors and not conditions.
Chronosystem	The *chronosystem* consists of all of the changes that occur over the lifetime of a person that influences their development, including major life transitions and historical events.	A child's parents getting divorced. A child being retained in the ninth grade.	

TOOL 5: PERSONAL CIRCLE MAP

How I want my educational ecosystem to feel for myself, the students we serve, and my colleagues.

The circle map is used for brainstorming ideas and showing prior knowledge of a topic, idea, or concept. For this exercise, you need three different colored pens or pencils.

1. In the center of a blank sheet of paper, write "Emotions at School."
2. Draw a circle around "Emotions at School."
3. Select one colored pen or pencil. Using this color in the area surrounding "Emotions at School," identify the emotions you want to feel when engaged in your work.
4. Select a second colored pen or pencil. Using this color in the area surrounding "Emotions at School," identify the emotions you want the students you serve to feel when engaged in learning and other activities at school.
5. Select the final colored pen or pencil. Using this color in the area surrounding "Emotions at School," identify the emotions you want your colleagues to feel when engaged in their work.
6. Identify themes across the emotions you identify for yourself, your students, and your colleagues.

After you have completed your circle map, respond to the following reflection questions.

7. What beliefs support these emotions in your classroom, school, or district?
8. What strategies can you identify to amplify these beliefs in your classroom, school, or district culture?
9. What beliefs inhibit these emotions in your classroom, school, or district?
10. What strategies can you identify to eliminate these beliefs in your classroom, school, or district culture?

TOOL 6: EDUCATIONAL ECOSYSTEM CULTURE TREE

Zaretta Hammond's Culture Tree depicts three levels of culture using the tree metaphor.

- *Surface culture*: The observable behaviors people share, such as holidays, food, music, language, talking styles, and dress, are depicted as the leaves on the tree branches.
- *Shallow culture* is represented by the trunk of the tree (as distinguished from surface culture, represented by the leaves and branches): The unspoken rules around everyday social interactions and norms—for example, social distance, eye contact, conceptions of time, or views about work.
- *Deep culture*: The roots of Hammond's Culture Tree represent deep culture. Deep culture is the beliefs, norms, and values that are shared among groups of people. In Hammond's representation of culture, the aspects of deep culture work together in what she identifies as the collective unconscious.

    1. Create a culture tree for your educational ecosystem. Your tree may represent a classroom, district, department, school, or another level of work that functions as an ecosystem. Be sure that each level of culture is represented on your tree.
    2. What does your tree tell you about the subconscious and conscious thinking in your ecosystem?

TOOL 7: BELIEF ASSESSMENT TOOL

Use the belief assessment tool to assess the evidence of each belief in operation in your classroom, school, or district. In the "Evidence" column, include information from the Pause and Process sections included in this chapter. In the "Growth" column, include areas where your ecosystem can grow in each belief area. In the "Strategy" column, identify at least one strategy to develop the opportunities you recorded for each belief area.

	BELIEF	EVIDENCE	GROWTH	STRATEGY
Black Lives Matter	Black Lives Matter is the unambiguous belief in the humanity, dignity, intelligence, beauty, and worth of Black people to our society and the planet. It is the belief that Black people, Black history, Black culture(s), Black experiences, and Black sensibilities are vital to the past, present, and future branches of the human family. It is the belief that Black people have the right to be everywhere and be vibrantly, joyfully, creatively, largely, and abundantly alive wherever we are.			
Belonging	"Belonging is the spiritual practice of believing in and belonging to yourself so deeply that you can share your most authentic self with the world and find sacredness in both being a part of something and standing alone in the wilderness" (Brown, 2019).			
Interdependence	Interdependence is the belief that people share social and emotional bonds with each other that support our individual and collective well-being and, at the same time, are allowed to hold a solid sense of self within these bonds.			
Empowerment	Empowerment is a multi-dimensional social process that helps people gain control over their own lives. It is a process that fosters power (that is, the capacity to implement) in people, for use in their own lives, their communities, and in their society, by acting on issues that they define as important.			

TOOL 8: ACTIONS TOWARD CULTURALLY RESPONSIVE-SUSTAINING EDUCATIONAL TRANSFORMATION (CRSET)

Referring to the ten principles of CRSET, identify one action you can take in your role and one action you can take in your education ecosystem in each of the ten principles of CRSET to spark CRSET.

PRINCIPLE	ROLE	ECOSYSTEM
Race and racism operate in all educational ecosystems.	Examine the policies and practices in my department for colorblindness and anti-Blackness.	Challenge the colorblindess and anti-Blackness I observe in the systems, policies, and practices in my school and district.
Culture influences our cognition, perceptions of the world, and how we learn.		
Leaders establish the systems, policies, practices, and culture structures that make CRSET possible.		
Affirming beliefs wire our educational ecosystems to recognize and tap into the genius of students, communities, and educators.	Ensure that lesson plans, curricula units, and other teaching materials integrate affirming beliefs into my instructional delivery. Plan for empowerment.	Participate in school and district curriculum writing so that I can champion and demonstrate how to align our instructional materials with affirming beliefs.
Educators need the resources, training, and support that personal and professional transformation requires.		
Educators' lives outside classrooms and schools matter to the learning that takes place inside them.		
Culturally responsive-sustaining competencies and methods empower educators to create powerful learning experiences.		
Educational experiences that sustain students' cultural, experiential, and linguistic knowledge propel learning.		
The social, historical, cultural, and political context of classrooms, schools, and districts must be understood and factored into the structures, policies, practices, and content that organize learning.	Learn from community leaders and elders about the history of my school's neighborhood and look for connections between local/state/federal policies and the school.	Connect my school's history to the history and experiences of other schools to identify systemic patterns.
All stakeholders work collectively to share information (data, strategies, experiences, reflections, etc.), learn together, build a common purpose, set goals, design plans, and hold each other accountable for using their collective power, knowledge, and resources to create change.		

References

Adiche, C. (2009). *The danger of a single story* [Video]. Ted Conferences. https://www.ted.com/talks/chimamanda_ngozi_adichie_the_danger_of_a_single_story?language=en

Allen, R. L. (2001). The globalization of white supremacy: Toward a critical discourse on the racialization of the world. *Educational Theory, 51*(4), 467–485.

Anderson, J. (1988). *The education of blacks in the South, 1860–1935*. The University of North Carolina Press.

Aronson, B. A., & Boveda, M. (2017). The intersection of white supremacy and the education industrial complex: An analysis of #BlackLivesMatter and the criminalization of people with disabilities. *Journal of Educational Controversy, 12*(1), Article 6. https://cedar.wwu.edu/jec/vol12/iss1/6

Aronson, B., & Laughter, J. (2016). The theory and practice of culturally relevant education. *Review of Educational Research, 86*(1), 163–206. https://doi.org/10.3102/0034654315582066

Au, W. (2023). *Unequal by design: High-stakes testing and the standardization of inequality*. Routledge, Taylor & Francis Group.

Baldassamo, C., Hasson, U., & Norman, K. (2018). Representation of real-world event schemas during narrative perception. *Journal of Neuroscience, 38*(45), 9689–9699. https://doi.org/10.1523/JNEUROSCI.0251-18.20

Baldwin, J. (1963). A talk to teachers. In J. Baldwin (Ed.), *The price of the ticket: Collected nonfiction 1948–1965* (pp. 325–332). St. Martin's Press.

Beiler, K. J., Durall, D. M., Simard, S. W., Maxwell, S. A., & Kretzer, A. M. (2010). Mapping the wood-wide web: Mycorrhizal networks link multiple Douglas-fir cohorts. *New Phytologist*, 185, 543–553.

Beiler, K., Simard, S., & Durall, D. (2015). Topology of tree-mycorrhizal fungus interaction networks in xeric and mesic Douglas-fir forests. *Journal of Ecology, 103*(3), 616–628.

Bell, D. (1992). Racial realism. *Connecticut Law Review, 24*(2), 363–379.

Belli, B. (2020, October 27). Racial disparity in police shootings unchanged over 5 years. *Yale News*. https://news.yale.edu/2020/10/27/racial-disparity-police-shootings-unchanged-over-5-years

Black Lives Matter. (2021, July 13). *9 years strong*. https://blacklivesmatter.com/8-years-strong/

Broader Bolder Approach to Education (BBA). (2022). Mission statement. https://www.boldapproach.org/index.html@p=2.html

Bronfenbrenner, U. (1992). Ecological systems theory. In R. Vasta (Ed.), *Six theories of child development: Revised formulations and current issues* (pp. 187–249). Jessica Kingsley Publishers.

Bronfenbrenner, U. (2005). The bioecological theory of human development. In U. Bronfenbrenner (Ed.), *Making human beings human: Bioecological perspectives on human development* (pp. 3–15). SAGE.

Bronfenbrenner, U., McClelland, P., Wethington, E., Moen, P., & Ceci, S. J. (1996). *The state of Americans: This generation and the next*. Free Press.

Brown, B. (n.d.). *The power of vulnerability* [Video]. Ted Conferences. https://www.ted.com/talks/brene_brown_the_power_of_vulnerability/transcript?language=en

Brown, B. (2019). *Braving the wilderness: The quest for true belonging and the courage to stand alone*. Random House.

Bryan-Gooden, J., Hester, M., & Peoples, L. Q. (2019). *Culturally responsive curriculum scorecard*. Metropolitan Center

for Research on Equity and the Transformation of Schools, New York University.
Buchanan, R. (2020). An ecological framework for supervision in teacher education. *Journal of Educational Supervision*, 3(1), 76–94. https://doi.org/10.31045/jes.3.1.6
Campbell, C. A. (1967). Towards a definition of belief. *The Philosophical Quarterly*, 17(68), 204–220.
Carter, P. L. (2018). The multidimensional problems of educational inequality require multidimensional solutions. *Educational Studies*, 54(1), 1–16. https://doi.org/10.1080/00131946.2017.1409225
Central High School (CHS). (2010). School improvement grant.
Civil Rights Data Collection. (n.d.). *LEA summary of selected facts*. Retrieved December 17, 2022, from https://ocrdata.ed.gov/profile/5/district/28404/summary
Coates, T.-N. (2015). *Between the world and me*. One Note.
Coleman, J. S., et al. (1966). *Equality of educational opportunity*. National Center for Education Statistics. https://files.eric.ed.gov/fulltext/ED012275.pdf
Comer, J. (1995). *School power: Implications of an intervention project*. Free Press.
Comrie, J. W., Landor, A. M., Riley, K. T., & Williamson, J. D. (n.d.). *Anti-Blackness/colorism*. Boston Center for Antiracist Research, Boston University. https://www.bu.edu/antiracism-center/files/2022/06/Anti-Black.pdf
Dalai Lama. (2010). *The universe in a single atom: The convergence of science and spirituality*. Harmony.
Davis, L. P., & Museus, S. D. (2019). What is deficit thinking? An analysis of conceptualizations of deficit thinking and implications for scholarly research. *NCID Currents*, 1(1). https://doi.org/10.3998/currents.17387731.0001.110
Data USA. (2023). *Camden, NJ*. Retrieved November 17, 2022, from https://datausa.io/profile/geo/camden-nj/#:~:text=In%202020%2C%20Camden%2C%20NJ%20had,%2428%2C623%2C%20a%205.95%25%20increase
DeMarrais, K. B., & LeCompte, M. D. (1998). *The way schools work: A sociological analysis of education*. Prentice Hall.
DiAngelo, R. (2017, June 20). No, I won't stop saying "white supremacy." *YES! magazine*. https://www.yesmagazine.org/democracy/2017/06/30/no-i-wont-stop-saying-white-supremacy
Doidge, N. (2015, February 6). Our amazing plastic brains. *The Wall Street Journal*.
Douglas, A. (1934). *Aspects of Negro life: From slavery through Reconstruction* [Digital Collections]. University at Buffalo Libraries. https://digital.lib.buffalo.edu/items/show/36410.
Douglas, F. (2020). *My bondage and my freedom*. Mint Editions.
Dumas, M. J. (2016). Against the dark: Antiblackness in education policy and discourse. *Theory Into Practice*, 55(1), 11–19. https://doi.org/10.1080/00405841.2016.1116852
Eccles, J. S., & Harold, R. D. (1996). Family involvement in children's and adolescents' schooling. In A. Booth & J. F. Dunn (Eds.), *Family–school links: How do they affect educational outcomes?* (pp. 3–34). Lawrence Erlbaum Associates.
Elflein, J. (2023, February 3). Distribution of Covid-19 deaths in the U.S. as of February 1, 2023, by race/ethnicity. *Statista*. https://www.statista.com/statistics/1122369/covid-deaths-distribution -by-race-us/
Elhoweris, H., Mutua, K., Alsheikh, N., & Holloway, P. (2005). Effect of children's ethnicity on teachers' referral and recommendation decisions in gifted and talented programs. *Remedial and Special Education*, 26(1), 25–31.
Elliott, S., & Davis, J. M. (2018). Challenging taken-for-granted ideas in early childhood education: A critique of Bronfenbrenner's ecological systems theory in the age of post-humanism. In A. Cutter-Mackenzie-Knowles, K. Malone, & E. Barratt Hacking (Eds.), *Research Handbook on Childhoodnature* (pp. 1119–1154). Springer, Cham. https://doi.org/10.1007/ 978-3-319-67286-1_60
Epstein, J. L. (2001). Building bridges of home, school, and community: The importance

of design. *Journal of Education for Students Placed at Risk (JESPAR)*, 6(1–2), 161–168.

Fergus, E. (2017). *Solving disproportionality and achieving equity: A leader's guide to using data to change hearts and minds*. Corwin.

Feuerstein, R., Feuerstein, R. S., & Falik, L. H. (2010). *Beyond smarter: Mediated learning and the brain's capacity for change*. Teachers College Press.

Freire, P. (2005). *Education for critical consciousness*. Continuum International.

Freire, P. (2010). *Pedagogy of the oppressed*. Green Bee.

Fullan, M., & Quinn, J. (2016). *Coherence: The right drivers in action for schools, districts, and systems*. Corwin.

Garvey, M. (1938). The work that has been done. *Black Man*, 3(10), 7–11.

Gay, G. (2018). *Culturally responsive teaching theory, research, and practice*. Teachers College Press.

Ginsberg, H. (1972). *The myth of the deprived child*. Prentice Hall.

Gooden, J., Hester, M., & Peeples, L. Q. (2019). *Culturally responsive curriculum scorecard*. Metropolitan Center for Research on Equity and the Transformation of Schools, New York University.

Gordon, D. M. (2010). *Ant encounters: Interaction networks and colony behavior*. Princeton University Press.

Gordon, D. M. (2014). The ecology of collective behavior. *Annual Review of Entomology*, 64(3), 1–16.

Gould, E., & Wilson, V. (2020). *Black workers face two of the most lethal preexisting conditions for coronavirus—Racism and economic inequality* (Report). Economic Policy Institute.

Grande, S. (2015). *Red pedagogy Native American social and political thought*. Rowman & Littlefield.

Guinier, L. (2004). From racial liberalism to racial literacy: *Brown v. Board of Education* and the interest-divergence dilemma. *Journal of American History*, 91(1), 92. https://doi.org/10.2307/3659616

Haddix, M., & Sealey-Ruiz, Y. (2012). Cultivating digital and popular literacies as empowering and emancipatory acts among urban youth. *Journal of Adolescent & Adult Literacy*, 56(3), 189–192.

Hammond, Z. (2015). *Culturally responsive teaching and the brain*. Corwin.

Han, S., & Ma, Y. (2015). A culture–behavior–brain loop model of human development. *Trends in Cognitive Sciences*, 19(11), 666–676. https://doi.org/10.1016/j.tics.2015.08.010

Hannah-Jones, N. (2021). *The 1619 project: A new origin story*. One World.

Hernández, T. (2023). *Racial innocence: Unmasking Latino anti-Black bias and the struggle for equality*. Beacon.

Hilliard, A. (1977). Classical failure and success in the assessment of people of color. In M. W. Coleman (Ed.), *Black children just keep on growing*. Black Child Development Institute.

Honig, M., Kahn, J., & McLaughlin, M. (2001). School community connections strengthening opportunity to learn and opportunity to teach. In V. Richardson (Ed.), *Handbook of research on teaching* (pp. 998–1028). American Educational Research Association.

hooks, b. (1994). *Teaching to transgress*. Routledge.

Howard, T. C. (2020). *Why race and culture matter in schools: Closing the achievement gap in America's classrooms*. Teachers College Press.

Hudson, M. J., & Holmes, B. J. (1994). Missing teachers, impaired communities: The unanticipated consequences of *Brown v. Board of Education* on the African American teaching force at the precollegiate level. *The Journal of Negro Education*, 63(3), 388–393. https://doi.org/10.2307/2967189

Ingersoll, R., Merrill, E., Stuckey, D., Collins, G., & Harrison, B. (2021). *Seven trends: The transformation of the teaching force* (Research Report). Updated January 2021. Consortium for Policy Research in Education, University of Pennsylvania.

Jackson, Y. (2010). *Pedagogy of confidence: Inspiring high intellectual performance in urban schools*. Teachers College Press.

Jensen, E. (2005). *Teaching with the brain in mind*. ASCD.

Johanson, D. C. (2004). Lucy, thirty years later: An expanded view of *Australopithecus afarensis*. *Journal of Anthropological Research*, 60(4), 465–486. https://doi.org/10.1086/jar.60.4.3631138

Johnson, M. (2012). *The 21st century parent: Multicultural parent engagement leadership strategies handbook*. Information Age Publishing.

Jones, D., & Hagopian, J. (2020). *Black Lives Matter at School: An uprising for educational justice*. Haymarket Books.

Jones-McGowan, E. J. (2011). *A case study of Dwight Morrow High School and the academies at Englewood: An examination of school desegregation policy from a critical race perspective* [dissertation]. The Graduate School–Newark Rutgers, The State University of New Jersey, Newark.

Kafele, B. (2019, September 2). *A deficit mindset has no place in a school* [web log]. Retrieved September 17, 2023, from http://www.principalkafelewrites.com/2019/09/a-deficit-mindset-has-no-place-in-school.html

Kendi, I. X. (2017). *Stamped from the beginning: The definitive history of racist ideas in America*. Bold Type Books.

Khalifa, M. A., Gooden, M. A., & Davis, J. E. (2016). Culturally responsive school leadership: A synthesis of the literature. *Review of Educational Research*, 86, 1272–1311.

Krulwich, R. (2016, March 9). The earth has lungs. Watch them breathe. *National Geographic*. https://www.nationalgeographic.com/science/article/the-earth-has-lungs-watch-them-breathe

Ladson-Billings, G. (1994). *The dreamkeepers*. Jossey-Bass.

Ladson-Billings, G. (2006). From the achievement gap to the education debt: Understanding achievement in U.S. schools. *Educational Researcher*, 35(7), 3–12. https://doi.org/10.3102/0013189x0 35007003

Ladson-Billings, G. (2014). Culturally relevant pedagogy 2.0: a.k.a. the Remix. *Harvard Educational Review*, 84(1), 74–84.

Lawrence-Lightfoot, S. (2004). *The essential conversation: What parents and teachers can learn from each other*. Random House.

Lee, C. D. (2008). Wallace Foundation Distinguished Lecture—the centrality of culture to the scientific study of learning and development: How An ecological framework in education research facilitates civic responsibility. *Educational Researcher*, 37(5), 267–279. https:// doi.org/10.3102/0013189x0832 2683

Lee, C. D. (2010). Soaring above the clouds, delving the ocean's depths. *Educational Researcher*, 39(9), 643–655. https://doi.org/10.3102/0013189x10392139

Lee, C. D. (2012). Conceptual and methodological challenges to a cultural and ecological framework for studying human learning and development. In W. F. Tate (Ed.), *Research on schools, neighborhoods and communities: Toward civic responsibility* (pp 173–202). Rowman & Littlefield Publishers.

Lee, C. D. (2017). An ecological framework for enacting culturally sustaining pedagogy. In D. Paris & H. S. Alim (Eds.), *Culturally sustaining pedagogies: Teaching and learning for justice in a changing world* (pp. 261–273). Teachers College Press.

Lett, E., Asabor, E. N., Corbin, T., & Boatright, D. (2021). Racial inequity in fatal US police shootings, 2015–2020. *Journal of Epidemiology Community Health*, 75, 394–397.

Levine, D. M., & Bane, M. J. (Eds.). (1975). *The "inequality" controversy schooling and Distributive Justice*. Basic Books.

Love, B. (2019). *We want to do more than survive: Abolitionist teaching and the pursuit of educational freedom*. Beacon.

Mapp, K. L., Henderson, A. T., Cuevas, S., Franco, M. C., Ewert, S., & Borrello, V. J. (2022). *Everyone wins!: The evidence for family-school partnerships & implications for practice*. Scholastic.

Maslow, A. (2013). *Theory of human motivation*. Martino Publishing.

Mediratta, K., McAlister, S., & Shah, S. (2009). *Community organizing for stronger schools: Strategies and successes*. Harvard Education Press.

Montagu, A. (2008). *Man's most dangerous myth: The fallacy of race*. Witley Press.

Morel, D. (2018). *Takeover: Race, education, and American democracy*. Oxford University press.

Morris, M. W. (2016). *Pushout: The criminalization of black girls in schools*. The New Press.

Morrison, K. A., Robbins, H. H., & Rose, D. G. (2008). Operationalizing culturally relevant pedagogy: A synthesis of classroom-based research. *Equity & Excellence in Education*, 41(4), 433–452. https://doi.org/10.1080/10665680802400006

Morrison, T. (1998). *Playing in the dark: Whiteness and the literary imagination*. Vintage Books.

Muhammad, G. (2020). *Cultivating genius: An equity framework for culturally and historically responsive literacy*. Scholastic.

Newark Board of Education (NBOE). (2020). *The next decade: 2020–30 strategic plan*. https://www.nps.k12.nj.us/info/the-next-decade/

Nilsson, B. (1998). An invitation to human ecology: Understanding environments, ecosymbolism and the change in the use for worlds. *Lund Archaeological Review*, 4, 19–28.

Noguera, P. A. (2008). *The trouble with black boys . . . and other reflections on race, equity, and the future of public education*. Jossey-Bass.

Noguera, P. A., & Wells, L. (2011). The politics of school reform: A broader and bolder approach for Newark. *Berkeley Review of Education*, 2, 5–25. https://doi.org/10.5070/b82110065

Oakes, J., Quartz, K. H., Gong, J., Guiton, G., & Lipton, M. (1993). Creating middle schools: Technical, normative, and political considerations. *The Elementary School Journal*, 93(5), 461–480. https://doi.org/10.1086/461735

Page, N., & Czuba, C. (1999). Empowerment: What is it? *Journal of Extension*, 37(5). https://archives.joe.org/joe/1999october/comm1.php

Paris, D., & Alim, S. (2017). *Culturally sustaining pedagogies: Teaching and learning for justice in a changing world*. Teachers College Press.

Payne, C. M. (2013). *So much reform, so little change: The persistence of failure in Urban Schools*. Harvard Education Press.

Perry, T., Steele, C., & Hilliard, A. G. (2003). *Young, gifted, and Black: Promoting high achievement among African-American students*. Beacon Press.

Picower, B. (2021). *Reading, writing, and racism: Disrupting whiteness in teacher education and in the classroom*. Beacon Press.

Pollock, M., Deckman, S., Mira, M., & Shalaby, C. (2010). "But What Can I Do?": Three necessary tensions in teaching teachers about race. *Journal of Teacher Education*, 61(3), 211–224.

Quinn, J., & Blank, M. J. (2020). Twenty years, ten lessons: Community schools as an equitable school improvement strategy. *VUE (Voices in Urban Education)*, 49(2), 44–53.

Race Forward. (2020, August 7). *Principles for racially equitable policy platforms*. https://www.raceforward.org/practice/tools/principles-racially-equitable-policy-platforms

Rogers, J. E. (2019). *Leading for change through whole-school social-emotional learning: Strategies to build a positive school culture*. Corwin.

Rosa, E. M., & Tudge, J. (2013). Urie Bronfenbrenner's theory of human development: Its evolution from ecology to bioecology. *Journal of Family Theory & Review*, 5(4), 243–258.

Safir, S., & Dugan, J. (2021). *Street data: A next-generation model for equity, pedagogy, and school transformation*. Corwin.

Schaeffer, K. (2022, September 28). *America's public school teachers are far less racially and ethnically diverse than their students*. Pew Research Center. https://www.pewresearch.org/topics/

Schwitzgebel, E. (2011). Belief. In D. Pritchard (Ed.), *The Routledge companion to epistemology* (pp. 14–24). Routledge.

Sealey-Ruiz, Y. (n.d.). Yolanda Sealey-Ruiz website. Retrieved September 7, 2022, from https://www.yolandasealeyruiz.com/

Seitz, R. J. (2022). Believing and beliefs—neurophysiological underpinnings. *Frontiers in Behavioral Neuroscience*, 16, 1–5. https://doi.org/10.3389/fnbeh.2022.880504

Seitz, R. J., & Angel, H.-F. (2020). Belief formation—a driving force for Brain Evolution. *Brain and Cognition*, 140, 105548. https://doi.org/10.1016/j.bandc.2020.105548

Seitz, R. J., Franz, M., & Azari, N. P. (2009). Value judgments and self-control of action: The role of the medial frontal cortex. *Brain Research Reviews*, 60(2), 368–378. https://doi.org/10.1016/j.brainresrev.2009.02.003

The 74. (2022, December 5). Schools face urgency gap on pandemic recovery: 5 takeaways from the new study. *The 74 Blog*. https://www.the74million.org/article/schools-face-urgency-gap-on-pandemic-recovery-5-takeaways-from-new-study/

Simard, S. W. (2015). Conversations in the forest: The roots of natures equanimity. *SGI Quarterly*, *79*, 8–9.

Simard, S. (2016, June). *How trees talk to each other* [Video]. Ted Conferences. https://www.ted.com/talks/suzanne_simard_how_trees_talk_to_each_other?language=en

Simard, S. (2017). The mother tree. In A.-S. Springer (Ed.), *The word for world is still forest* (pp. 67–69). K. Verlag Press.

Solorzano, D. G., & Huber-Perez, L. (2020). *Racial microaggressions: Using critical race theory to respond to everyday racism*. Teachers College Press.

Sousa, D. A. (2017). *How the brain learns*. Corwin.

Span (2009). *From cotton field to schoolhouse: African American education in Mississippi, 1862–1875*. The University of North Carolina Press.

Spring, J. (2018). *The American school: A global context from the Puritans to the Trump era* (10th ed.). Routledge.

Stacker. (2022, January 20). *Cities in New Jersey with the most living in poverty*. Stacker. https://stacker.com/new-jersey/cities-new-jersey-most-living-poverty

Steele, C. M., & Aronson, J. A. (2004). Stereotype threat does not live by Steele and Aronson (1995) Alone. *American Psychologist, 59*(1), 47–48.

Stovall, D. (2016). *Born out of struggle: Critical race theory, school creation, and the politics of interruption*. State University of New York Press.

Sugiura, M., Seitz, R. J., & Angel, H.-F. (2015). Models and neural bases of the believing process. *Journal of Behavioral and Brain Science*, 5(1), 12–23. https://doi.org/10.4236/jbbs.2015.51002

Tatum, A. W. (2009). *Reading for their life: (Re)building the textual lineages of African American adolescent males*. Heinemann.

Tenenbaum, H. R., & Ruck, M. D. (2007). Are teachers' expectations different for racial minority than for European American students? A meta-analysis .*Journal of Educational Psychology*, *99*(2), 253–273.

Thurman, H. (1980, May). *The sound of the genuine. Baccalaureate graduation, Spelman College*. Retrieved October 17, 2022, from https://thurman.pitts.emory.edu/items/show/838

Trungpa, C., & Lief, J. L. (2010). *The heart of the Buddha: Entering the Tibetan Buddhist path*. Shambhala Publications.

United States Zipcodes. (2023). *Cities in ZIP code 07423*. Retrieved December 27, 2022, from https://www.unitedstateszipcodes.org/

Valenzuela, A. (1999). *Subtractive schooling: Issues of caring in education of U.S.-Mexican youth*. State University of New York Press.

Villegas, A. M. (2007). Dispositions in teacher education: A look at social justice. *Journal of Teacher Education*, 58(5), 370–380.

Vygotsky, L. S., Cole, M., Stein, S., & Sekula, A. (1978). *Mind in society: The development of higher psychological processes*. Harvard University Press.

Warren, M. R., & Goodman, D. (2018). *Lift us up, don't push us out!: Voices from the front lines of the Educational Justice Movement*. Beacon Press.

Weber, M. (2002). *The Protestant ethic and the spirit of capitalism*. Penguin Classics.

Wells, L., & Noguera, P. (2012). Comprehensive urban school reform for Newark: A bolder and broader approach. In E. J. Dixon-Roman & E. W. Gordon (Eds.), *Thinking comprehensively about education: Spaces of educative possibility and their implications for public policy* (pp. 243–258). Routledge.

Wilkerson, I. (2021). *Caste: The origins of our discontents*. Thorndike Press Large Print.

Index

CORWIN
A Sage Company